THE
POWER
OF GOD'S
WORD

BY

REV. JOSUE YRION

© Copyright 2004 by Josué Yrión
Josué Yrión World Evangelism & Missions, Inc.
P.O. Box 876018
Los Angeles, CA. 90087-1118
United States of America
Fax (562) 947-2268
Phone (562) 928-8892
E-mail: josueyrion@josueyrion.org
Website: www.josueyrion.org

Published by:
Ebed Press
3103 Villa Avenue
New York, NY. 10468
United States of America
Website: www.ebedpress.com

Credits:
Cover design by: Colin Smith
www.pixeloverload.com

ISBN: 0-9741927-9-1
Library of Congress Control Number: 2004105174

Printed in the United States of America

Contents

"Do your best to present yourself to God as one approved, a workman who does not need to be ashamed and who correctly handles the word of truth"

2 Timothy 2:15—NIV

"As ministers of the Gospel, there is nothing more extraordinary than to hear another preacher speak his or her message, without veering away from the subject, following the same thought throughout the introduction, body and conclusion of the message; and that the preacher be genuine, a person of integrity, of wisdom and powerful in the knowledge of Scriptures. That the speaker be learned in homiletics and hermeneutics, a person of power and authority, and above all the humility to admit that his or her ministry belongs to God and that the Lord is not using his or her life because of personal eloquence or theological education."

(Extracted from Rev. Josué Yrión's sermon given in the City of Kristiansand, Norway, on August 1998)

Presentation

In this book Rev. Josué Yrión impresses two of the key principles of his ministry: his passionate love for Christ and his radical commitment to the truth of God's Word. When you read "The Power of God's Word" — undoubtedly true and loyal to the biblical revelation — you will be challenged to fully commit yourself to the unchangeable principles of God's Word. You will be inspired to live a victorious Christian life, full of victories and the anointing of the Holy Spirit. This book will bring a holy unrest into your heart. Some may find the truths of this book to be very radical, while others will be affected or maybe pricked with some of the assertions. However, those who read this book with a prayerful spirit, and are open to the work of the Holy Spirit, will be greatly blessed and awakened to live an exciting Christian life, with the desire to increase Christ's Kingdom through the power of God's Word.

Dedication

Above all, I dedicate this literary work to the Lord Jesus Christ. Only He knows the effort, the yearning, and the passion that I deposited into its pages to become a reality in the middle of so many trips, crusades, and the physical exhaustion that these activities bring about. I thank God that He led me to preach these messages — now part of this book — that have blessed thousands of people. I'm certain that these sermons will also bless those who read through the pages of this book. This is why I dedicate my first book to God, because only He is worthy of my praise, glory, and honor for all eternity.

Secondly, I dedicate it to my loving wife Damaris, my helpmeet of great wisdom and spiritual discernment, and faithful companion in the ministry who has collaborated with her wisdom, prayer life and words of encouragement. Damaris, if it weren't for you, I wouldn't have been able to finish this book.

Thirdly, I want to dedicate this book to my beloved children: Kathryn and Joshua Yrión Jr., whom lovingly and with great abnegation, have understood my ministry as an evangelist. They know about my calling, the travel it involves, and the absence from home it requires to carry on such an important labor. Thank you Kathryn and Josue for always receiving me with hugs and kisses, I have also cried because of the distance that so many times keeps us apart. And being half around the world has kept me from being with you on your birthdays and other special holidays to hug you.

I also dedicate this book with all of my heart to my dear parents: Jesus Pujol and Maria Ione Minussi, who have taught me in the ways of the Lord from my childhood; and supported me in everything when God called me to the ministry.

Finally, I want to dedicate this book to all believers or non-believers who are seeking a God-opportunity to change their lives through the knowledge that only the Word of God, the Bible, can give. As you read the pages in this book you will find the true peace that is only found in Christ because the Lord has inspired them and because they are based on the Bible, the book that reveals the foundation for the redemption of man.

Only the Bible can show a person the way to repentance, forgiveness, regeneration and justification through Jesus Christ, the true God, by His shed blood on the cross of Calvary. I pray that as you read this book you recall the words of the Apostle John:

> *But these [things] are written that you may believe that Jesus is the Christ, the Son of God, and that by believing you may have life in His name.*

John 20:31 NIV

This finished work is an old-dream fulfilled that was born many years ago. This is why I dedicate it to all the above mentioned with all of my heart, soul and spirit.

Rev. Josué Yrión
Los Angeles, California
January 2004

Foreword

Jesus' main emphasis was the preaching of God's Word. All His messages pointed in one direction: the need to repent and to change radically in all the aspects of practical life, teaching us that words take us nowhere unless there is a change in the listeners attitude.

Jesus could speak of many subjects to a select group of people, whom after hearing His words were perplexed by the message and in which manner Christ presented them.

We know that Jesus, as a preacher, was more committed to His Word and to the message than to what his oratory represented, or a recognition given by a select group of listeners.

In a time when there was a lack of character, Jesus introduced the principles of a new lifestyle. His favorite messages, if I may say so, can be found frequently in different situations, like in Matthew 18:4, Luke 14:11 and 18:14. These messages are a divine warning to those who desire and extremely yearn to be important. The Scriptures declare:

"For whoever exalts himself will be humbled, and whoever humbles himself will be exalted."

Matthew 23:12

Every word that Jesus uttered had a commitment with truth. Many times the Pharisees tried to catch Jesus in His words to find fault in Him, but they never found anything in Christ' attitude that would compromise the integrity of His life and His message.

We are now living in a very special time in where a great number of new preachers of the Gospel of Christ are emerging. The Church of Christ is full of great men of God of remarkable theological expression, prepared academically, experienced in the use of the pulpit, that with eloquent messages can make us weep of emotion. Undoubtedly, they are great preachers. However, a question arises, "Are we following Jesus' example, as ministers of God, living the Word that we preach, and being entirely committed to His Word?"

A foreword for a book with this title is to me of great answerability. At least its twofold: First of all, am I the right person to do it? And secondly, does the author have the integrity to back up his work? The fear to such an awesome and Holy God makes us tremble. Nevertheless, I do it humbly, without merits or for vainglory, only by the grace of the Lord Jesus Christ. And also because I am committed with God's Word, and with the servant and author of this book whom I've known over twelve years, and I know that his life of integrity, sustained by the Lord, can back up what he is written. I can also testify of his humbleness and his fear of God. The emphasis of this book truly is The Power of God's Word. The title clearly expresses everything and challenges us to discover our responsibility with the Holy Scriptures, the Bible. This book shows us that God continues to be the same as always: Faithful to His Word!

The messages in this book, which have already been preached from the pulpit, will be a powerful point of reference for thousands of people that desire to commit themselves to the Scriptures. It's my prayer that God blesses those reading this book and that the power of the Holy Spirit fills your heart with holy fear and a burning desire to live-out, without doubts, the spiritual principles contained in God's Word.

Pastor Wilmar Silveira
International Director for
Josué Yrión World Evangelism and Missions, Inc.
Lodi, New Jersey, January 2004

Chapter One

God's Eternal Source

One time when Kathryn was two and a half years old and Josué Jr. was one, they were playing in the living room. All of a sudden, Junior took Kathryn's doll and ran off with it. She went after him and said, "Give me my dolly back", and snatched the doll away from little Junior. Once more, he took her doll and ran off with it. Kathryn ran after him and recovered it again. As if this were not enough, Junior seized the doll a third time and ran away from Kathryn. Then Kathryn, a little more irritated, came close to Junior and, staring him in the eye, said, "Junior, in Jesus name, give me my doll back." My little son complied and left. Kathryn went up to my wife Damaris and said, "Mom, there is power in the name of Jesus, there is power in the name of Jesus!" The power in Jesus' name is the theme that I will share with you through this book. Prepare your heart to hear God's voice, as we submit to His word.

A fundamental need

Undoubtedly, today we need to return to God's Word. The Church needs to return to the power of God's Word. Pastors need to return to the preaching of God's Word. The writer of the book of Hebrews declares:

> *"For the Word of God is living and active. Sharper than any double-edged sword, it penetrates even to dividing soul and spirit, joints and marrow; it judges the thoughts and attitudes of the heart"*

> Hebrews 4:12 NIV

The Scriptures declare that God's Word is alive. It was alive yesterday; it's alive today and for all eternity. God's Word is neither outdated nor modern, but eternal. Many churches around the world have been negligent in the preaching of God's Word by teaching doctrines and other philosophies other than those in the Bible. We now need to return to His teachings, His wisdom, and His power.

While visiting the City of Madras, India, some seventy thousand people attended our crusade, and six thousand seven hundred souls accepted Christ as their Savior.

During the first night, the Lord restored the sight of a blind woman. The second night, a paralytic began to walk on the platform. We saw amazing signs and wonders. Why? Because God's Word, the simple gospel of the cross was preached. God's Word changed these Hindu people and transformed the lives of thousands of others as well. It destroyed and shattered the devil's power. This is what the awesome power of God's Word does. The Scriptures validate and confirm that it's alive. But now a question arises: What is God's Word?

The uniqueness of the Bible

Thousands of years ago, a book began to be written that would endure the most cynical criticism of its enemies, and the most meticulous examination carried out by the most brilliant minds of the earth. The Bible endured, during those years, many foes and all the imaginable attacks of its critics around the world. In spite of everything, the Bible continues to be the best seller of all ages, the unbeaten champion, who is friend to millions of people that found peace, spiritual well being, and the assurance of eternal life.

In my travels to Arab, Muslim, socialist or communist countries, or even to the Buddhist countries of Asia, I have seen how many of these cultures have attempted to destroy God's Word. But they have never succeeded and they never will succeed, and never will. Thousands strived to ridicule the Word of God, but their endeavor has been, and will be in vain. Day after day, the Bible is the book most sold and read in the world. What is the indisputable secret to the triumph of God's Word? Will there be a day in which its influence will die off, losing its power?

In 1985, I visited all the feared communist countries behind the Iron Curtain: Poland, Czech Republic, Hungary, Rumania, Bulgaria, Yugoslavia, and the former USSR. I felt and saw the great need that our brothers had to have a Bible. While, in the West, Bibles are full of dust and forgotten by a many Christians; behind the Iron Curtain, millions of people desire a Bible to share with their family. Even today, in the Asian communist countries (The Bamboo Curtain) such as: China, North Korea, Burma, Vietnam, Cambodia, Laos, etc., thousands of Christians are being imprisoned, tortured, executed and killed simply for the "crime" of having a copy of the Bible, God's Word.

Recently, thousands of Bibles sent to Cuba from the United States, were burned by the local government. The soldiers of Fidel Castro's communist regime put fire to the Bibles at the "Managua military unit", in the municipality of "Arroyo Naranjo", under the pretext that the books were "subversive". Eyewitnesses reported that thousands of Bibles were thrown from a truck into a hole in the ground and burned. The Bible covers read: "Cuba for Christ". The government did not agree with the title, because they believed it should have read: "Cuba for Fidel". The communist government of Cuba has endeavored to destroy God's Word for at least forty years. Thirty years ago, in one event, they burned one hundred thousand Bibles, and later another twenty-seven thousand more. However, Fidel Castro will never be able to destroy what God has established. For it is written:

> *"...I will build my church, and the gates of Hades will not overcome it."*

(Matthew 16:18)

A Fascinating Book

The Bible is the most fascinating book ever written. Just in 1968, one hundred ten million five hundred thousand copies were distributed. The Bible is found all over the world and it's been translated into approximately twelve hundred and fifty languages. A London newspaper published an article about the extraordinary sales volume of Bibles stating, in that year alone, that Bible sales exceeded those of the top ten selling books, sold in Great Britain during the last ten years! What wealth we find in God's Word! When we consider these facts, undoubtedly a question comes to our mind: What is the Bible? How has it endured so many centuries withstanding the attacks of critics and enemies and still conserved its power and authority? What is the foundation of its admirable influence, and why have so many people read it, loved it, and faithfully followed its commandments? Why have so many given their lives for the Bible before denying its truth and infallibility? How is it that it possesses such a special power to direct man's life in righteousness, integrity and moral values? Why have kings, presidents, governors, statesmen, doctors and professionals, as well as common people, given the Bible a distinctive place in their libraries? Why have wise men, scholars of literature and scientists searched the Bible seeking to find a source of inspiration for their works? What is the Bible?

> *The Bible possesses God's supernatural power. Its sentences have come from the lips of the Most High. Its words are not those of men, as the Apostle Peter stated in his second letter: "Above all, you must understand that no prophecy of Scripture came about by the prophet's own interpretation. For prophecy never had its origin in the will of man, but men spoke from God as they were carried along by the Holy Spirit."*

II Peter 1:20,21 NIV

The Bible has no contradictions or human errors. Scripture is perfect because it does not contain the words of men, but God's Word in written format. Usually, when someone buys a medicine bottle, there is a label that states: Warning or Drug Interaction Precaution. It can say: "Do not take this medicine if you are allergic to any of the drugs contained in it" However, the Word of God is apt for anyone to use. Everything written in the Bible is perfect; there are no errors, and you need not take precautions. Hallelujah! This is the power of God's Word. The Bible is and always will be the eternal Word of the Divine and Powerful: the foundation for morality and decency, the spiritual guide and compass for life's decisions.

The Bible is a Source for Revelation

God has revealed himself to man through His Word. Christianity is not a religion in the commonly understood sense. The word religion comes from the Latin word "religare." It means to unite man and God. This is what religions try to do, but it's always through human efforts. Man could never and cannot go to God by himself. Religion, broadly speaking, is the useless effort of man trying to reach God by his or her own ways or works. Christianity is based on the fact that God sent Jesus Christ to the world to save man, by taking our place and dying on the cross of Calvary. This is what the Apostle Paul states in his letter to the Ephesians:

> *"For it is by grace you have been saved, through faith—and this not from yourselves, it is the gift of God—not by works, so that no one can boast.*

Ephesians 2:8,9 NIV

The Bible is simple and specific. You can believe what it says about the work of the cross, and be saved while you are reading it. You can be healed of your sicknesses and at the same time be filled with the power of the Holy Ghost. All you need to do is believe in God's Word as the only source of faith and authority for your life, then you need to surrender your life to Christ, and He will write your name in the Book of Life. The Bible states in the Gospel of John:

> *"In the beginning was the Word, and the Word was with God, and the Word was God."*

John 1:1 NIV

In verse eleven of the same chapter it states that Christ "came to that which was his own, but his own did not receive him." God revealed himself to man through His incarnate Word, even Christ, who is God's eternal Word to man.

The greatest power in the world is not the power of bombs and missiles, strong armies and supersonic aircrafts, the large tanks and enormous sea carriers, or the political power of Washington or any other world power. The greatest power in the world today is God's Word; He is the only true God and after Him there is no other. When we preach the Word with power and authority, God will change, transform, save and restore the people who believe in the power of His Word. Personally, I have preached this Word from Alaska to Chile, from Spain to Japan, in all of the continents and in at least seventy countries around the world, and to this moment, I have never lost an argument. The Word has never suffered defeat; its enemies have never been able to triumph over it. Quite to the contrary, I have always exalted it as a good soldier of Christ, I have always preached it with simplicity, but also with the power and the anointing of the divine authority vested in my life. When I'm on the pulpit I can hear—as D.L. Moody used to say—"another voice, that of the Holy Ghost".

The Bible is a Source of Literature

The Bible is the most credible source of literature in the world, by virtue of its excellent writings. In the Bible's pages, we find the Book of Job, considered to be the first drama known in history, and the Book of Psalms, which is the most ancient poetic collection in the world. Its literary treasure resides in both its topics and in the quality of the writing. Many of the poets and writers of Rome and ancient Greece were immoral people, corrupt, sensual and perverse. Consequently, the topics they chose for their work reflected who they were. In their writings were false and ridiculous religions, wars, and ambitious fanatics, full

of lust and sensuality that attempted to destroy the whole-
ness of the family, and incited the worship of strange
pagan gods, that are condemned by God's Word.

The writings of the Bible are holy and pure promoters
of life and perfect love. The Hebrew writers, inspired by
God, were men of a holy lifestyle and pure of heart. Their
inspired writings were those of happiness and the well
being of man and family. These men proclaimed His perfection and divine attributes in their writings. These were
holy, humble and God fearing men. They wrote extraordinary words that changed thousands of lives throughout
history. This is the power of God's Word. The Hebrew
poets were the most sublime men in their nation. Among
them were kings of high character, judges of great integrity, renowned heroes and legislators whose fame has
reached the uttermost parts of the earth. They include
Moses, David, Solomon, Job and others.

A young Czech once said: "A missionary that came
here gave me a Bible scripture, it was a very small piece of
paper, very small. I began to love that scripture, memorized it, and studied it day and night". This young man
walked very happy throughout the streets of his country
because he had in his hands a Bible scripture. This happened when the Czech Republic was under communist
rule. Observing this young man's attitude, his pastor said:
"You can't go around the streets shouting, Glory to God!
Glory to God! We are in a socialist country and the
authorities will have you arrested for that." Hearing what
his pastor said to him the young man replied, "The piece of
Scripture that the missionary gave me said, 'And the Word
of the Lord came to Jeremiah, and if Jeremiah received a
Word from God, a Word from the Lord can come to me".
You must love God's Word, read it, study it, obey it, and

believe it with all of your heart. There is no other book on the face of the earth like the Bible.

In 1985, when I was in the city of Athens, in Greece, I went up to the Areopagus, the place where Paul preached to the philosophers, epicureans, and stoics; from that place I was able to observe the Acropolis and the Pantheon, the symbols of Athenian wisdom, the place from which Plato, Socrates and Epicurus discoursed. What has come to be of the Acropolis and the Pantheon today? Where are the Greek philosophers that wrote their works and spoke of greatness? Dust; everything has been reduced to dust and forsaken. Their great auditoriums and theaters are stones full of dust from much trampled ground. Everything is over. Compare the human glory to the majesty of God's Word: "The grass withers and the flowers fall, but the word of our God stands forever" (Isaiah 40:8) this is the difference between the human and the divine writings.

The Bible is a Source for History

Among the sources for history the Bible is a true treasure. For this reason many historians have used it to obtain invaluable historic information. The Bible not only gives us an excellent and well organized account of Hebrew history in detail, but also gives important information about other important ancient civilizations: Egypt, Persia, Media, Babylon, and Rome. There are many truths historians would never have learned without the Bible. There was a time that historians doubted the Bible as a source of history. However, through archeological discoveries, they began to see that the Bible was right. To this day, nothing can be proven against the historic events recorded in the Bible. There isn't a university, a professor, or an intellectual that would dare doubt the Bible as a source of wisdom and authority, in regard to historical events recorded in the pages of the Holy Scriptures; which are powerful, profound and infallible.

Currently, archeological magazines in the U.S. have credited the Bible for their recent discoveries. An example of these is the discovery of a skeleton found in the Philistine City of Askalon, Israel. The cranium had an orifice in the middle of the forehead, and it was considered to be just like the one Goliath had. Just think of the impact this discovery had on those who don't believe in God's Word: the atheist and agnostics; when the Jerusalem Archeological Museum exhibited to the world the skeleton and the skull which they believe was that of Goliath of Gath, according to the Biblical account in the Book of the Prophet Samuel.

The Bible is a Source of Redemption

What is redemption? It's liberty! It consists of the premise that someone pays the price that you should have paid for your crime, setting you free. In Christian redemption, someone has already paid such a price, one that you would never have been able to pay. The Bible says that Christ redeemed us when He died on the cross at Calvary. He gave His life for us. If He wouldn't have given His life, we would be eternally lost without salvation. But He paid the price to save our souls, to heal our diseases and to write our names in the Book of Life.

In the letter to the Ephesians, Paul speaks to us about the redemption we receive through Christ:

"In him we have redemption through his blood, the forgiveness of sins, in accordance with the riches of God's grace"

(Ephesians 1:7 NIV)

Not only does the Bible reveal God's love, righteousness and holiness, but it also shows us the spiritual need we have to return to Him. It reveals our fall and it offers the remedy to our spiritual disease: The Blood of the Lamb of God, Jesus Christ. God reveals himself to man through the pages of the Bible and reaches the pinnacle of that revelation in the person of Jesus Christ. The main message of the Bible is: God came to man through the birth, life, death and resurrection of His Son Jesus Christ.

It is said that when slavery was common practice in the U.S., a ship from Africa arrived at the coast of Georgia. Those who were in the slave trade were waiting in the marketplace where the slaves would be presented and auctioned. Many owners of large parcels of land, used mainly for agriculture, were there to buy the slaves for the hard, difficult and heavy labor of the fields. However, in the midst of all the trading of dark-skinned human beings, a man of fine attire arrived on scene. Staring at one of the slaves for sale, he cautiously examined his mouth, his legs, his arms, his back, and addressing the man that kept him tied on a log, in the middle of the marketplace, said, "What's the price for this slave?" The answer became evident in the expression of the slave owner's face, indicating a large sum of money. Nevertheless, in a calm and gentle manner, he reached for his wallet and a sack of gold and silver coins, and placed them in the slave owner's hand, and said: "I'll take him. I like him!" Immediately, the slave was handed over to him. As soon as he took possession, with affection he took the chains off the slave's hands, feet, and neck letting them fall on the ground and, to everyone's surprise, he said: "Now you are free! I have bought your liberty for a very high price that you were not able to pay. You can go now; you were bought and are now free, I redeemed you from slavery and from the misery of chains and prison. You are free forever"

This is exactly what Christ did for us. He paid the price; made us free, unshackled us from the chains that had us imprisoned, delivered us from the prison of our sins and let us go free from guilt. He redeemed us. Hallelujah! So it is that millions of people seek help through the Bible in times of desperation, frustration, confusion and anguish. People from all over the world have found, in the Bible, the source of redemption in the person of Christ, and have obtained peace and salvation for their souls.

When Napoleon was exiled in the island of Santa Elena, after reading the New Testament, he said, "I was leading a revolution using the force of war, swords, shields and javelins, but reading the pages in this book I discovered that Christ made a greater revolution than mine, without violence or destruction. He unleashed the revolution of love and spiritual liberty, through the blood he shed on His cross." What does the Bible mean to you? Have you taken time to read it during the year? What does it represent to you and your family? How much of your day do you dedicate to study God's Word to discover the power of the Scriptures?

The Bible is a Source of Inspiration

A young man was preparing his luggage to go to the university, where he would stay four years. Arranging his belongings he left an empty corner in his suitcase. As his friend was watching him fix his suitcase, he asked him what he was planning to put in that empty spot. The young man hastily replied:

—I'm going to put a flashlight, a hammer, a sword, a map and a mirror.

His friend exclaimed:

—That's impossible! There's no way you can fit all that in your suitcase!

To what the young man responded:

—In this little corner of my suitcase I'm going to put my Bible; which is all that and much more.

Hallelujah! That young man, going into a hostile setting, like our present day universities are, found inspiration in the Word of God.

Understanding that the Bible has sixty-six books, written throughout centuries by different authors, and considering that such authors lived in different times and locations; we come to the conclusion that only God could have inspired these men. Some of the Bible's authors were kings, statesmen, prophets, legislators, soldiers, generals; others were farmers, war heroes, and lawyers. We also find that a shepherd, a poet, a tax collector, a doctor, the beloved disciple, and a simple fisherman, wrote some of the texts. In addition, we learn that a knowledgeable multilingual apostle was included in the texts. When we look closely, we can learn that all of these authors were in line with the same message, in perfect coherency, down to the last detail throughout thousands of years. We then arrive at the conclusion that only a divine, extraordinary, and perfect mind could have inspired these men. Altogether they pointed to the same and only theme: The Messiah Redeemer, Christ Jesus, who was to come to the world.

Let's suppose that we pick sixty-six of the best-written medicine books of the last five hundred years that would have been written by forty independent specialists on the same subject, for example, the treatment of a specific disease. If we would bind all those books into one book, do you believe that all forty doctors would talk about the same subject? Impossible! Taking into account the advancement of technology, each doctor, considering his own time, would say something different due to the progress of medicine. Here lies the difference between the Bible and common books. All the biblical authors pointed in the same direction; there is no other book like that. The best writings of medicine or science have become outdated in the last twenty years. However, the Bible is the only book that can preserve itself at the same pace of progress.

For this reason, the Bible holds world leadership in history and culture. Whatever you need to find in another book, look it up in the Bible; it's already there. Knowing that God's Word is unique in every way is a great inspiration. It's an incomparable, fascinating book; there is no work on the face of the earth that can be compared to it. There has never been and never will be a book like it. The Bible is the Book of books, absolute, indestructible and invincible. Marx, Stalin, Lenin and Mussolini have passed away. Where are they? Generations come and go, empires arise and fall. Where are they? The Word of God is still with us. And with it we will conquer the gates of hell. The Apostle John says:

> *"I write to you, young men, because you are strong,
> and the word of God lives in you, and you have overcome
> the evil one."*

1 John 2:14b

Knowing that we have conquered through the Word is a source of inspiration.

Some years ago, at the University of Massachusetts, a group of doctors discovered that our tongue controls the whole body, and all our actions and attitudes through the central nervous system. How curious! Science of our day discovered something that the Book of James declared two thousand years ago! What a source of inspiration we find in the Bible! It goes ahead of technology and human progress. The Bible is eternal!

Whatever you read tomorrow in the paper — The New York Times, or any other publication — is already in the Bible today. We already knew of the false peace agreements between the Jews and the Arabs. We already knew that the peace agreement that President Bill Clinton signed with Syria would have no effect. We know that the world is preparing itself to receive the Antichrist. And we also know that soon the heavens will open, the trumpets will sound, and the Church will be caught up to be with Him forever. Hallelujah! Adrian: do you think you can get this quote as it originally appeared...I assume in English..—scg E.M Goodchild said, *"The Bible is the only book that entirely satisfies the needs of all men, and inspires them to live a full life. The Bible was of vital importance to those men who lived thousands of years ago, and is of the same importance to modern man. It is to the advantage of every man, either from the east or west, from the cold regions of the north or the warm regions of the south. It delights children and never wearies the old. The ignorant is able to understand it; the wise and educated are bewildered by it. It's gainful to the scholar, the philosopher, and the poet to help them finish their works more profoundly, finding inspiration in the divine pages."* Finally, the main subject in man and his relationship with God; its objective is salvation for lost souls, and its consequences are eternal.

A Separate Place for the Bible

You can have a library, as I have mine. However, put the Bible in a place separate from the rest of the books. As Rui Barbosa said, *"If I place it beneath the rest of the books, it will sustain the ones on top; if I place it in the middle, it will be the heart of those books, and if I place it on top of the books, it will be the head and authority of all the books in my library."* Dr. Van Paul Kenger once said, *"I still don't understand half of the glories in the Bible, even having studied it for over forty years, day and night. When the Bible's wisdom is depleted, I will have time to read works such as Shakespeare or Goethe; for the time being, I will read it again during the next forty years..."* D.L Moody said, *"I thought that if I would pray faith would come like lightning, but I learned that faith comes by hearing, and hearing by the Word of God"* Richard Wurmbrand said that the Bible sustained him during his prison years for the Lord's sake. He wrote the book entitled *Tortured for Christ.* Our Baptist brothers of the former USSR and China have given their lives for Christ. Why do they do it? What drives them to die for Christ? What sustains them during that time? It's the knowledge of God's Word! We could burn ninety percent of all the books in the world, but if we gave a copy of the Bible to each child in the world, we would have a courageous-God-fearing-honest-morally upright-full-of-integrity generation of men and women.

As a result of man's sin and disobedience, the unbeliever have launched a fuming attack against the teachings of the Bible. But they haven't been able to dim any of its pages. World powers have conspired against it, but they have not been able to destroy it. The Bible has been contested, ridiculed, scorned and publicly burned. It was censored like no other book, but it remains strong as steel, breaking the hammerheads of opposition. It's a great inspiration to know that no one can, or will be able to destroy it. Every system, philosophy, false religion and cult, have criticized the Bible with every kind of attack and violence to discredit it. However, every one of these, without exception, has been put to shame by the authority and the power of God's Word. It's the only book that has been read in every nation of the world. The United States was established on the basis of God's Word. England was founded on the principles of God's Word. This is why these nations are so rich and powerful. Quite to the contrary, in Latin America and the African countries we can see poverty and misery, in the material realm as well as the spiritual realm. As Christians, the Bible is to us as the air we breathe; it is our daily bread, and the water we drink. We cannot live without it.

Our children, Kathryn and Josué Yrión Jr., have been, and are taught in a daily fashion the Word of God. Damaris, my wife, reads the whole Bible with them once a year, while I fulfill my calling to evangelize traveling all over the world. She is a wonderful woman of God, as her father was, an extraordinary man of God and pastor in Cuba; he is now gone to be with the Lord.

William T. Ellis wrote a lovely poem describing the Bible in the following way:

With the Holy Spirit as my guide, I have entered the pages of this wonderful book that we shall call the Bible. I came in through the portico of Genesis and walked through the art gallery of the Old Testament. There I saw the depictions of Abraham, Isaac, Jacob, Joseph, Moses, David, Solomon, Isaiah, Jeremiah and Daniel hanging on the wall. I crossed the threshold into the music hall of the Psalms, and the Spirit of God placed His fingers on the keys of my nature, until it seemed that each musical cord elevated itself to God's throne, responding to David's harp and the enchantment of king Solomon's poetry. Then I come into the observatory of the prophets and saw pictures of different sizes; which were stars of things that were to occur, surrounding a huge Star that would arise in expiation for sin. Then I entered the King of kings' chamber of audience and saw it from four perspectives: Matthew, Mark, Luke and John. Then I went into the place of the Acts of the Apostles and saw the Holy Spirit forming a Church. Thereafter, I entered the hall of letters and saw Paul, Peter, James and Jude writing their Epistles to the world. Entering the throne room of God, I saw a door at the bottom of the tower. While going up, I found someone standing, bright as the morning sun. It was Jesus, the Son of God. Ending in Revelation, I saw him in His full Glory, and He taught me the way of life and He showed me this Book, the Bible; it would teach me to live and die for Him.

What a tremendous inspiration to hear these words about the Bible! Yes, the Bible is a source of inspiration for all.

The Bible is a source of Treasures

At age eleven, John Wanamaker, the prince of American businessmen, bought a copy of the Bible. Many years later, referring to that purchase he said, *"It's clear to me that during my life I have made purchases in the millions of dollars. However, when I was a child of only eleven years, I made the most important purchase of my life when I bought a small red cover Bible for $2.75 in monthly installments. Considering my past, I see that small red cover Bible, founded and shaped my life from my youth making me a clean, honest man of integrity in the business world. Now I understand that investment was the greatest and most precious purchase that I've ever made.. It set the founda-*

tion of my character and personality for the rest of my life; in the private sector as well as in the professional." Undoubtedly, John Wanamaker was right; the Bible is the most valuable asset that any person can buy.

One day, on a U.S. television interview show, the host introduced five young ladies between the ages of twenty and twenty-three years old, who had been examined by a gynecologist to confirm that they were virgins. They had been invited to participate in this program to talk about sex out of marriage. The presenter ridiculed and laughed at their point of view, because they said they would remain virgins until they got married. The public was divided. Most of the audience favored the television host, questioning how it was possible that they were still virgins at that age, considering the time we live in. In the midst of this debate, one of the young ladies invited to the program opened her purse and took out a Bible. Looked at the host, and said with a firm voice full of authority: *"I don't care if you are a pervert, if your son is a drug-addict or if your daughter is a prostitute; in fact I don't care what you say or think. My father is a pastor, and he taught me to remain a virgin until the day of my marriage. This book I hold in my hands is called the Bible. Its contents have taught me the moral values of respect and holiness, that neither you, your family or this public possesses."* Everyone remained silent and ashamed before the words this young Christian lady, full of wisdom, said about the power of God's Word.

The precious treasure of this young lady was in the Scriptures. Where is your treasure? Does the Bible have a precious place in your life?

George Muller, from Bristol, England, said at one

point that he had read the whole Bible over 100 times. And referring to the Scriptures he said that it was the greatest and most precious asset in his life and that the Holy Scriptures was the reason for his success in his personal and ministry life. Dear reader, how many times have you read the Bible? How much of your daily time do spend reading it? Does it have an important part in your life?

The Bible says that God's people are destroyed for lack of knowledge; Bible knowledge is the source and the secret to a victorious life in every aspect. Come back to the Bible! Return to its teachings! The absence of a careful study of the Scriptures is the main reason why so many false doctrines and cults, pseudo-churches and misleading ministers are rampant today. All this happens for the simple reason of not knowing the Bible, its power and final authority in our life. It's impossible for you to have an appropriate knowledge of God without knowing what the Bible says. God is in the pages of this precious book.

The Bible is a source of Knowledge

One time we held a crusade in Volta Redonda, Rio de Janeiro, Brazil. The first night I emphasized the call to churches and ministers to return to God's Word. Brazil needs to return to God's Word. During the four days of the crusade there was an attendance of eighty-five thousand people. Seizing the opportunity I stressed several times that Rio de Janeiro needs to return to God's Word. I preached about the need for a Biblical revival and stated that the revival would come when we returned to the Scriptures. There are many people who are scholars of science but are illiterate when it comes to the Divine Scriptures. Intellectualism without God becomes ridiculous, as the Bible states in the letter to the Corinthians:

> *"Brothers, think of what you were when you were called. Not many of you were wise by human standards; not many were influential; not many were of noble birth. But God chose the foolish things of the world to shame the strong. He chose the lowly things of this world and the despised things — and the things that are not — to nullify the things that are, so that no one may boast before him."*

1 Cor 1:26-29 NIV

This text teaches us that human wisdom without God is vain, foolish and ridiculous before the Creator. Look at how Jesus replied to the Sadducees who boasted of themselves and the wisdom they possessed:

> *"You are in error because you do not know the Scriptures or the power of God"*

Matthew 22:29 NIV

Here is the heart of the message in this book: without the knowledge of God, of His word and the power of Scriptures we cannot survive in a world that belongs to the evil one. Come back to God's Word! Hear the call of the Spirit! Begin reading, loving and studying the Scriptures! It's the only way; there is no other way!

The knowledge of the Bible is the most valuable treasure you can obtain in this life! It is the foundation for the ministry; it is the base for a holy, upright life, and a relationship with God. It is the foundation of the Church; it's the foundation for marriage, for the young, for the man and the woman. It is the foundation for your personal and professional life, as it has been for the family today and always.

The Bible has the knowledge about anything you desire to learn. It's an open book that contains all the wisdom, about any subject, that your mind desires to find out. In the XVI century, during the reign of Edward VI of England, a bishop named Hoover examined three hundred eleven priests, to prove if they really knew the Scriptures. Many simple questions were asked, for example writing out the "Lord's Prayer". In correcting the answers, it was proven that out of the three hundred eleven priests, sixty six did not return their answer pages; ten did not know the "Lord's Prayer" by heart (something of uttermost importance for a priest); twenty-seven did not know who the author was; thirty did not know in what part of the Scriptures it was written; and one-hundred-sixty-eight could not explain the importance of the prayer that Jesus taught.

Once a certain preacher was speaking about the 'Coming of Christ' and said to the people: "Jesus, talking about His return, said that His return would be after one-thousand-years but that two-thousand would not pass..." The pastor, sitting on his platform chair, struck by the preacher's statement exclaimed: *"Jesus didn't say that!"* To which the preacher replied: *"If He didn't say it, He must have, because the prophecies are being fulfilled."* Although this incident might seem funny, a person can be spiritually ignorant when he does not know the Scriptures.

The devil knows if we know the Scriptures and the power of God's Word. As we can read in Matthew chapter four, the devil himself used the Scripture to tempt Jesus. He tempted Jesus using God's Holy Word. The Lord Himself spoke about the importance of knowing the Scriptures when He said:

"Study diligently the scriptures; because you think

that by them you possess eternal life. These are the Scriptures that testify about me." (John 5:39 NIV footnote)

A philosophy professor at one of the greatest universities in the United States prepared an exam for one hundred students, for the purpose of measuring their biblical knowledge. He wrote nine simple and easy questions. Out of the one hundred students, four did not return their answer sheets; and of the remaining ninety-six, only eight responded correctly to all of the questions; eighty-eight were not able to find the Book of Jude. Men like Jeremiah, Solomon, Daniel, and the Book of Leviticus were identified as the judges of Israel. Matthew, Mark, Luke and John were considered prophets, while Herod, Ananias and Nebuchadnezzar were thought to be kings of Israel. One of the students said that the Pentateuch was the same thing as the Gospels. This will give just a little idea of the crisis we face today. There is a lack of biblical knowledge in huge proportions; which has become a destructive power to this generation. The remains will be debris and ashes of what we used to be: a people who knew, respected, feared, and had great reverence towards God.

Making plans for a wedding, the best girl friend of the bride asked for the opportunity to read a verse of Scripture from the Bible during the ceremony, to which the bride agreed, because they'd been friends since childhood. On the wedding day, in front of the altar, to everyone's surprise, instead of reading 1 John 4:18 (NIV) *"...but perfect love drives out fear"*. She read from the Gospel of John 4:18 where Jesus spoke to the Samaritan woman: *"the fact is, you have had five husbands, and the man you now have is not your husband"* Can you imagine the commotion and the uproar she caused as a result of lacking knowledge of the Scriptures? It's true that an occurrence as this can provoke laughter in all of us; however, it underscores the real lack of Bible knowledge in our churches.

There are two words in Latin to define *"word"* in the Scriptures. One of them is *"logos"*, which means the written Word of God. The second one is *"rhema"* which means the revealed Word of God. When you receive the *Rhema of God*, no one will be able to destroy you. Allow God to reveal to you His Word! He wants to have daily fellowship with you.

On a certain occasion, D.T. Niles said: *"Men who talked with God and received the Divine Revelation wrote the Bible. When we pray we talk with God; but when we read the Bible, God talks to us."* We can say as Whitehead said many years ago about what's in the Scriptures: *"The Bible contains God's thoughts, the state of man, the way of salvation, the condemnation of sinners, and the happiness of Christians. Its doctrines are holy, its precepts are just, the stories are true, and its instructions are unchangeable. Read it to be wise, believe in it to be saved, and practice it to be holy. The Bible contains the light for direction, food for sustenance, and comfort to bring joy. It's the travel map, the staff of the pilgrim, the pilot's compass, the sword of the soldier, and the Christians manual. In it, paradise is restored, the heavens are opened, and the doors of hell are restrained. Christ is its theme, our good is its purpose, and God's glorification is its goal. Read its pages carefully in prayer. It's a mine of riches, a paradise of glory, and a river of pleasure. It rewards he who reads it, condemns he who takes it for less, and defeats all of its enemies.*

To conclude I want to highlight that Christ is the Bible's central message. He is the main subject in each Book of the Bible. In the Old Testament, in the Book Genesis, Christ is the seed of the woman; in Exodus, Christ is our Passover; in Leviticus, Christ is our expiatory sacrifice; in Numbers, Christ is our Rock, column of fire during the night and cloud during the day; in Deuteronomy, Christ is the prophet that is to come; in Joshua, Christ is the Grand General; in Judges, Christ is the Great and only True Judge; in Ruth, Christ is our closest relative; in the Books of Samuel, Kings and Chronicles, Christ is our King by excellence; in Ezra, Christ is Scribe, learned in the word; in Nehemiah, Christ is the wall builder, He who restores our life; in Esther, Christ is our Lawyer; in Job, Christ is assurance of victory in trials and tribulations; in Psalms, Christ is the all in all in our lives; in Proverbs, Christ is our wisdom; in Ecclesiastes, Christ is of uttermost importance in our lives because everything apart from him is vanity; in Song of Solomon, Christ is the Rose of Sharon, the Lily of the Valley, the Husband of the Bride, and the Chosen One among ten thousands; in the prophets from Isaiah to Malachi, Christ is the Messiah of Israel and He who would come to save our soul from sin and judgment, and the one who would fulfill all the prophesies throughout His birth, life, death, and resurrection. Christ opens the pages of the New Testament and in Matthew, Christ is King; in Mark, Christ is the Servant; in Luke, Christ is the Son of Man; in John, Christ is the Son of God; in Acts of the Apostles, Christ is the one who pours out the anointing of His Holy Spirit; in Paul's Epistles, from Romans to Philemon, Christ is He who puts everything under His feet, and is the Head of the Church; in the general epistles of Hebrews, James, Peter, John and Jude, Christ is the absolute ruler of our faith, holiness and conduct in the Church; and, in Revelation, Christ closes the Scriptures as the Alpha and Omega, the beginning and the end, the first and the last, the King of kings and Lord of lords, the faithful and just, and He who was, who is, and is to come, the Almighty."

Many have sought help in the Bible and found it to be a source of revelation: this is awesome. Many have found it to be a source of literature, others, a source of history, which is extraordinary. There are those who have found a source of redemption, which is glorious. And many others have found it to be a source of inspiration, which is admirable. There are even those that have found in it a source of treasures: this is wise. And many others regard it as a source of knowledge, which is profound, great and eternal.

Chapter Two

The Power of God's Word

During the 1993 earthquake in California, where we live, something humorous happened to our family. When the floor began to shake at about 4 a.m., we ran out of our rooms. My wife Damaris took hold of Kathryn's arm, and I got Junior out of his room. Kathryn was about three and Junior one and a half years old. My daughter was crying in Damaris' arms due to the shock and saying over and over: "The housie belongs to Jesus, Mommy, the housie belongs to Jesus, Mommy..." I confess that I was the most nervous one of all four of us, for I walked from one end of the house to the other shouting, "Hear the girl, Lord! Hear the girl Lord! The housie belongs to Jesus." Then, my wife and I took some oil, anointed the children, and walked through the house anointing the doors and windows, asking the Lord to protect us from the earthquake's destruction We hadn't heard the news yet. But later we learned that the earthquake had been so strong that train cars and vehicles had rolled over, buildings had collapsed, and long stretches of street were destroyed. We clearly saw that God had protected us with His power. When we finished anointing the children and the house, I put away the oil bottle. My little daughter Kathryn saw where I placed the bottle, so the next day, silently, she grabbed a chair, reached into the kitchen cabinet, and took the bottle of oil in her hands. Then she called Junior over to her and opened the oil bottle. However, instead of putting a few drops of oil on her finger, she anointed Junior by pouring the entire contents over his head. You couldn't imagine how slippery our kitchen floor was!

Kathryn ran to her mother and said: "Look mommy, Junior is anointed! Junior is anointed!" This may seem funny to you, but I was the one who cleaned the kitchen floor and slipped in the process. Children... What a gift from God!

> *"Therefore this is what the Lord God Almighty says: 'Because the people have spoken these words, I will make my words in your mouth a fire and these people the wood it consumes"*

Jeremiah 5:14 NIV

The Bible is God's eternal source. It is a fountain of revelation, of literature, of history, of redemption, of inspiration, a fountain of treasures and never ending knowledge. These are the subjects I will share with you in this chapter. We will examine the efficacy of the Word, its warmth and its infallibility. The Word of God is unique. It's unlike any other book: impossible to imitate or clone.

In March of 1993, our ministry conducted a crusade in the City of Moscow, the former Soviet Union where we took sixteen thousand Bibles. We received a special invitation to speak at the Soviet military base that was near the Kremlin. Nine pastors came with me on a humanitarian-diplomatic visa. We were able to take Bibles, and, after the service, distribute them to the soldiers and officers of the Russian army. The base was situated beside the Red Square, the place where the old Lenin mausoleum is located. We preached God's Word with simplicity and authority and two hundred fifty Russian soldiers surrendered their hearts to Jesus. The major and commander of that military base, Pishik Osip Viachesla Vovich, also accepted Christ and asked to say a word. His eyes welled up with tears as he spoke: *"What the socialist and communist system could not do in seventy three years, God did it tonight. When I heard the Word, my soul and my heart were converted..."*

Hallelujah! Damaris, my wife, was crying-happy watching how the soldiers received Christ. In fact, the whole staff was crying as they watched the wonderful power of God's Word in action.

The Major's life was changed in such a way that he asked if we would leave the Bibles so that they could be distributed to the soldiers and officers at other military bases in Russia. What a wonderful experience to see the tears of these men, the expression of joy on faces that had been transformed by the power of God's Word! This is what the Bible can do: it can transform, regenerate, clean the heart, and save it.

From there we traveled to Kiev, in the Ukraine, where we distributed eight thousand Bibles. The spiritual thirst in that town moved our hearts deeply. I preached in an auditorium that was used in the past by the Ukrainian Communist Party. Behind the curtain you could just barely see the statue of Lenin, degraded and full of dust. I was deeply touched to see about one thousand seventy people fill the place and remain standing for two and a half hours of service. What a thirst they had for God and His Word! When I began to preach, I did it as always, with simplicity and power. A woman blind in one eye was healed instantly by the power of God after hearing the Word. As soon as the service was over, the beloved Ukrainian people were pressing in, hugging us, some even kissing us as an expression of affection.

A woman, taking her Bible, put it on her chest and shouted: "Forty years ago Stalin took my Bible away, but now I got it back, I got it back!" And with tears in her eyes she said, "I don't want money, I don't want clothes, I don't want anything else but God, I want the Word of God!" What a powerful experience to preach in Moscow and Kiev! It was amazing to see how these Russians and Ukrainians received the Bibles we distributed with such incredible love. In 1942, when Stalin was at the Kremlin watching the Soviets march to war he said, "Here in the Red Square, of Moscow, communism will bury Christianity!" Isn't it marvelous that all the members of our staff, holding each other's hands, prayed in the Red Square many years later, proclaiming the opposite of the words that Stalin uttered? We were there, and communism had fallen behind the Iron Curtain. Contrary to the words of Stalin, Christianity buried communism in the Red Square of Moscow. Who triumphed? Was it the words of a man called Stalin or the powerful Word of God?

Observing the appalling former KGB building, we praised God because what used to be the headquarters of the Soviet Secret Police has become today the Russian Bible Print shop. Who would ever imagine this? Where are God's enemies? Where is Marx, Lenin, Stalin or Brejner? And where is Christ? Christ inhabits the midst of His people by His Holy Spirit and is seated at the right of the Father clothed in glory, power, majesty and authority forever.

1 — The Power of Influence of God's Word

a. The Word of God is like a consuming fire:

"I will make my words in your mouth a fire, and these people the wood it consumes."

Jeremiah 5:14 NIV

As I preach God's Word, I'm totally aware of the power it has to burn rebellious hearts and take them to repentance by the Holy Spirit. It purifies the most intimate thoughts that anyone can have, and it can dissipate the guilt with which someone may be burdened on the inside. Its power in the spirit realm is so great that we will never understand it entirely.

During a crusade we conducted in Madras, India, the Hindu priests would face us, invoking the power of the devil to destroy us. But all of their efforts were useless. The power of the Word consumed every lying sign that the enemy tried to harm us. During the second night they tried to stone us but God caused a heavy rain to fall and they had to leave in shame.

India is a dark nation and closed to the Gospel in which satanic hosts have blocked the minds and souls of tens of thousands of peoples, putting them in bondage to misery and spiritual ignorance that has dragged them to worship: rats, cows, and serpents as gods. There are some thirty million "other gods" in a population of one billion people, out of which eighty three percent are Hindu, eleven percent Muslim, and only two percent Christian. To this day, India has been one of the greatest challenges for our ministry. It's an extremely poor, filthy and miserable country. Many people defecate in the streets, and when people die their bodies are burned and the ashes thrown in the river, leaving a horrible flesh stench in the air that many times caused us nausea. You can't drink the water, the air is difficult to breathe, and the food is not edible. The three weeks we were there, the Lord delivered us from disease and the attacks of the enemy. We overcame by the power of God's Word, which acted like a consuming fire, influencing many hearts unto salvation, transforming lives, and healing those afflicted by disease. Hallelujah!

Some time ago, an Australian missionary and his two sons sleeping in their Jeep were burned alive after they had ministered in a very hostile area of India. Pray for the missionaries to India!

b. The Word of God is like a Demolishing Hammer

> *"'The one who has my word, speak it faithfully. For what has straw to do with grain?' declares the Lord. 'Is not my word like fire,' declares the Lord, 'and like a hammer that breaks a rock in pieces?'"*

Jeremiah 23:28-29 NIV

The Bible has power to obliterate the devil's power, destroying and shedding into pieces all his evil works. It's not only a consuming fire, as we've seen before, but it's also a hammer, used to shed? the enemies intentions against us, when it's ministered in wisdom and anointing.

No one can love a god that one doesn't know. The Hindus serve gods that they don't know. We can truly love God only if we know Him, something that is possible only through His Word. It's a sledgehammer available to you for the destruction of any barrier that the devil puts in your way.

When God's Word is preached, it's a fire that burns and purifies the human heart. It's a sledgehammer that shatters sin and human pride. It's the sword that cuts and plucks out guilt and resentment out of the human heart.

c. The Word of God is a force that imparts life

> *"So I prophesied as I was commanded. And as I was prophesying, there was a noise, a rattling sound, and the*

bones came together, bone to bone. 'Come from the four winds, O breath, and breathe into these slain, that they may live.' So I prophesied as he commanded me, and breath entered them; they came to life and stood up on their feet –a vast army.

Ezekiel 37:7,9,10 NIV

In crusades around the world, I've seen innumerable healings and miracles take place on behalf of those who there was no hope. What's impossible for medicine is possible with God. The Scriptures clearly state: *"I am the Lord, who heals you." Exodus 15:26*

The Word has power to solve your problems, those that are humanly impossible to solve and seem to have no solution. I've observed conflicts in marriages at the point of divorce that were worked out through the power of the Word. People at the verge of divorce surrendered their lives to Jesus and He helped them giving them peace, restoration and reconciliation. Many brothers approached me, or my wife, to ask us to pray for their wayward child. Sometimes I hear parents say: "There is no hope or change for my son, his case is lost!" And then after a few weeks or months, they come back to share with us that their child was saved and restored by God, when they (as parents) resolved to believe in the Word; to believe that it has the power to give life even to those who seem dead, lost and hopeless to the human mind.

When D.L. Moody heard Spurgeon preach at the London Metropolitan Tabernacle, he put his head between his hands and, on his knees, he said he never heard a man preach like that, with authority in the Word giving life to everything he said.

"Particularly, I would say that there's nothing like listening to a good preacher who correctly handles the Word of truth, and feeds the Word into the hearts of His people.

Sadly, there are many preachers that who fables and funny stories, which have become a waste of time to the saints. We haven't been called to tell fables, or to use our preaching time to criticize other ministries. We have been called to impart life through the preaching of the Word to those who listen."

Every time I preach, be it in the U.S, to a tribe in Zaire, in a metropolis like London, in a rich country like Japan or a poor place like India, I keep in mind that there are people lost in sin, in prostitution, in drugs, in broken marriages, lives destroyed by such a variety of causes. Then what I do is preach God's Word as it is. At any place, in any country, the need in the human heart is the same, and so is the answer: hear and believe the Word of God that gives life and life more abundantly.

d. The Word of God is powerful in everything

"In this way the word of the Lord spread widely and grew in power."

Acts 19:20 NIV

The Word of God has power of influence because it has all power. It's not only powerful but powerful in everything! This Scripture reads that it spread widely and grew in power. When we hear the Word and believe it, we grow spiritually and prevail against the attacks of the enemy. A minister who preaches the Word faithfully will see his Church expand greatly, growing in both membership and power.

At the Central Baptist Church of Peking, China, there is a Bible chained to a post. The Chinese brothers sign their names on a list that is on a mural many months in advance just to have the opportunity to read some scriptures for a few minutes. Every day, at the Peking Baptist Church, there is a huge line of believers patiently waiting to read the Scriptures, and in moments as those, many weep with a burning heart for God's Word. They possess such love for the Scriptures that they don't want to stop reading them and give way to the other brethren. What a thirst for God's Word! What a difference in reality compared with other people who, having access to the Scriptures, do not read or meditate in the Word.

It could seem difficult for you to imagine a scene such as I just mentioned, and feel moved by it, because what the eyes don't see, the heart can't feel. However, the Word of God has been powerful in the lives of our Chinese brothers, sustaining and strengthening them in the midst of the persecution they suffer.

Recently, we traveled to China and, thank God, today there are more Christians than Communist party members in the country. Hallelujah! God is faithful!

Sadly, the latest Church research done in the United States revealed that more than seventy seven percent of church members don't know the books of the Bible in the order they are placed. This is ridiculous! That's why there is so much sin and immorality in our churches; we don't know the Bible as we should. While Oriental Christians are dying every day for the sake of the Scriptures, persecuted because of their faith, Western Christians are dying every day for lack of knowledge in the Scriptures. What an irony!

e. The Word of God has power for salvation

"I am not ashamed of the gospel, because it is the

power of God for the salvation of everyone who believes."

Romans 1:16a NIV

The Word of God has great influence because it has power for salvation. When someone hears the gospel of power, based on the authority of God's Word, and believes it, the Holy Spirit will convict that person of guilt in regard to sin and righteousness and judgment, so that the person repents and becomes saved.

The Book of Romans states that it is "the power of God unto salvation". The word *"power"* is translated from the word *"dunamis"*. Here the word *"power"* or *"dunamis"* has the sense of dynamite — explosive or bomb... Hallelujah! That's what God's Word is!

Angels cannot preach the Word because they have no testimony, nor have they experienced salvation. Nevertheless, this awesome privilege was given to us: to preach the mysteries of the Gospel of Christ. The reason for this is that Christ has redeemed us, washing us with His blood and cleansing us by His Word. Hallelujah!

f. The Word of God is a weapon

Take... the sword of the Spirit, which is the word of God.

Ephesians 6:17b NIV

The Word has influence because it is an offensive weapon. A sword, in contrast with a shield, is not a defense weapon but an attack weapon. Therefore, the sword is not a defense weapon, but to attack, to invade, to fight, to win and take possession of that which God has for each of us. For that reason, we must use it with power. In the Book of Acts, we find twenty-seven instances in which the Apostles preached the Word with "boldness", "daringly" and with courage.

In the Czech Republic, there was a pastor that preached during a whole year with only one Scripture of the Bible. Each time he would go to preach, the Lord would give him a new message out of the same Scripture he had used many times over. God said to him that he didn't need to make notes, or elaborate an outline of what he was going to preach; for He was going to give him a new inspiration out of the same Scripture for each new occasion. Hallelujah!

During one of my visits to the Communist countries, I was able to observe that many brethren traveled huge distances by foot to obtain a Bible or a page of some book, or even just one verse of Scripture to exchange with the other believers. They would say: "Brother, would you trade with me this Scripture out of Matthew that I have, for one out of Luke or John? Or the Old Testament, for I have many out of the New Testament."

There were those who said to us that the only literature they had of the Bible were some of the Billy Graham sermons that they heard over short wave radio in their country. They would copy some of the sermons by hand and then use them as weapons of attack when they faced their circumstances of being persecuted. What a thirst for God's Word!

When we buy a microwave or a new refrigerator, along with the appliance we get an instruction manual to properly operate the appliance. The Bible is our manual; it will guide us into eternal life. Follow its instructions and you will reach your destination!

g. The Bible is a probe

"For the word of God is living and active. Sharper

*than any double-edged sword, it penetrates, even to divid-
ing soul and spirit, joints and marrow; it judges the
thoughts and attitudes of the heart..."*

Hebrews 4:12 NIV

The Bible examines us; it probes our heart and all the
realms of our life. A probe, technically speaking, is a piece
of lead tied to a rope that is used to measure the depth of
water or to explore the deep. In the same manner, in our
spiritual life, the probe of God's Word knows, recognizes,
and is able to evaluate every aspect of our human nature.
It knows every realm of our life. A probe can also be a
huge apparatus for perforations that reaches great depths
and is used to conduct ground and soil surveys. The Word
of God is a spiritual probe that reaches into the depths of
the human heart, to the point of knowing each detail of a
thought, sentiment, idea or deed.

Remedy for the Soul

In medical science, a probe is a rubber tube that is
introduced in the cavities of a body to examine the state of
the patient, extract retained fluids or to introduce some
liquid substance, be it medicine or food. The Word is a
probe that is introduced into the mind, the heart, the soul,
and the spirit of man, to make him or her see the nature of
their state of sin. The Word of God penetrates like a powerful and mighty probe into the most intimate realms of
our being to introduce the medicine that heals the soul.
This same probe produces conviction of sin as well as the
spiritual nourishment to grow, mature, and to mold the
Christian character in the life of those whom have received
Christ. Just like a medical probe would extract retained
fluids in an organism of someone who is ill, God's Word

extracts what is retained — keeping you back — in your being. It pulls out any thought, word or deed that is not in tune with God and His Word, taking you into a personal relationship with your Creator. How beautiful!

A probe is also used for recognition of different terrains and their depths in a geographical area, and the water depths in a hydrological survey. In the medical field, it's also used to determine the depth of a wound caused in an accident. In the same manner, God's Word is powerful to recognize the depth of the human heart, anything hidden in the terrains of our childhood, or even sad and bitter experiences that we may have had in life. The Word will measure the depth of the turbulent waters of our past sin and remove all guilt, taking away the feeling of emptiness from our heart. It heals every wound caused by words that have been pronounced against us in our past. It has the power to remove any root of bitterness or unforgiveness from the heart. It can also erase the unpleasant memories of our childhood, adolescence and youth. Let God's Word "probe" your heart.

2 — The Power of God's Word to Stand Firm

"Your word, O Lord, is eternal; it stands firm in the heavens."

Psalms 119:89 NIV

We usually say: "Time passes by quickly!" Time does not pass, we are the ones that pass by quickly; God remains and we pass. Paul, on a certain occasion, said to his disciple Timothy: *"...But God's word is not chained"* (2 Timothy 2:9). God's Word has no limits; it is not chained or limited to time, and it's impossible that anyone could imprison or enslave it with the purpose of impeding that it be preached and proclaimed. In 1993, after one of the crusades we held in Russia, I took my wife Damaris to visit Italy. When we arrived at the Coliseum, in Rome, our minds traveled two thousand years back in time to visualize the scene in which Caesar, the emperor, threw the Christians into the arena to be eaten by the lions. Hundreds of men, women, and children gave their lives for Christ as the hungry beasts of the Roman Empire devoured them. They destroyed hundreds of human lives but they were not able to destroy the spreading of God's Word; which was later preached throughout the Empire. Next, we visited the prison where the great Apostle Paul was beheaded for Christ' sake. While there, we felt God's presence; and looking at those walls that two thousand years ago had imprisoned the Apostle, we hugged each other and cried and, on our knees, we thanked God because His Word was not chained, but expanded throughout Europe. And on our knees, we prayed that God would strengthen us, and give us wisdom and power to finish our ministry faithfully, unto that day that we hear: "Well done, good and faithful servant! Come and share your master's happiness". Hallelujah! Praise His Name!

Rome is full of suffering: the incarcerations, the tortures, and the blood of Christ' martyrs, but the Word was never chained, they were never able to silence it. God is faithful!

> *"…The word of our God stands forever."*

Isaiah 40:8 NIV

In 1985 when I traveled to Istanbul, Turkey, I tried to obtain a visa to go into Iran, because there was a World Islamic Conference taking place. Unfortunately, I was unable to obtain it. The Ayatollah Khomeini proclaimed some words against Christianity and the Bible during the conference. Here is my question: Where is the Ayatollah now? He's gone! Where are those that in the past were God's foes? They don't exist! However, God's Word stands forever. Jesus speaking of His word said:

> *"I tell you the truth, until heaven and earth disappear, not the smallest letter, not the least stoke of a pen, will by any means disappear from the Law until everything is accomplished."*

Matthew5:18 NIV

On a different occasion, Jesus, referring again to the nature of His Word, said: "Heaven and earth will pass away, but my words will never pass away" (Matthew 24:35 NIV) Christ is not a affiliated with the powerful political parties of the United States, the Democrats nor the Republicans. Jesus is Lord! He is the King of kings and Lord of lords. His term is not limited to four years. He reigns and He reigns forever. The Apostle Peter also repeats this truth:

> *"But the word of the Lord stands forever. And this is the word that was preached to you."*

1 Peter 1:25 NIV

On one occasion a missionary in San Pietro, Italy, gave a Bible to a builder. The builder, with the intention of ridiculing the missionary, hid it in a wall, taking one of the bricks out and placing the Bible in the cavity. Then he covered it with cement and marked the place with a cross. Later on, when the missionary asked him where the Bible was, lying to her, he said that he was reading it. Some months later, there was a big earthquake in San Pietro. The builder, seeing so many buildings destroyed, recalled the Bible he had hidden. So he ran to the construction site and noticed that three of the four walls had fallen, and only one remained standing. Then, coming close to the wall, he thought: Is this the wall where I hid the Bible? Coming closer, he saw the cross on the wall, and removing the brick, to his surprise, there was the Bible, intact, just as he had placed it. The other walls had fallen to the ground, except the one in which he had hidden the Bible. Hallelujah! His Word is indestructible; no one will ever do away with it. Praise God for His wonderful Word!

The human mind cannot understand the reality of eternity. Our mind is not able to comprehend the magnitude and the depth of the word "eternity". To be able to understand eternity, imagine with me a mountain made of iron and steel with a height of 10 miles, and length of 10 miles, and a width of 10 miles. Now imagine along with me that every one hundred years, a bird poses on the top of this iron and steel mountain, scraping its beak two times, and then flies away. After one hundred years, it comes back and on the very top of this huge mountain of iron and steel with a height of 10 miles, a width of 10 miles, it scrapes its beak two times. That's only a second in eternity. Do you understand? Eternity is something that escapes our understanding. The Bible says that there are two places where you can spend eternity: heaven or hell. Heaven is the place for those who received Christ as their savior and lived according to His power. Hell is a place for those who reject Christ, His salvation and His Word, living for the pleasures of the world and their own flesh, only to satisfy their sinful passions. Where will you spend eternity? The Bible says the Christ' Word is eternal. It has no end. Hallelujah!

How can a man or a woman commit adultery knowing that God will judge them? How is it possible for someone to change the glory of God for the glory of men? How can someone put to risk their life, and soul, living in sin, instead of repenting and surrendering to Jesus? How can someone reject the free gift of salvation and prefer to live in accordance to worldly pleasures that only last a short season? The Bible says that their sin will catch up to them. Jesus himself, speaking of this, declared:

> *"There is a judge for the one who rejects me and does not accept my words; that very word which I spoke will condemn him at the last day."*

John 12:48 NIV

Accept Jesus today! Run to Him now!

3 — The Nourishing Power of God's Word

> *"He humbled you, causing you to hunger and then feeding you with manna, which neither you nor your fathers had known, to teach you that man does not live on bread alone but on every word that comes from the mouth of the Lord."*

Deuteronomy 8:3 NIV

Through the Gospel of Matthew, we know that the devil used God's Word against the Lord Jesus Himself. Satan knows that God's Word has power and he used it to tempt the Christ. "The tempter came to him and said: *'If you are the Son of God, tell these stones to become bread'* Jesus answered, *'It is written: Man does not live on bread alone, but on every word that comes from the mouth of God.'"* (Matthew 4:3-4 NIV)

The devil would say: "It is written" But Jesus would answer: *"It is also written"* Jesus defeated him by the Word.

We can also defeat devil. Hallelujah!

In the Word, we can read about Job's declaration: *"I have not departed from the commands of his lips; I have treasured the words of his mouth more than my daily bread."* (Job 23:12 NIV) The Word of God has power to nourish us spiritually and to usher us into an abundant life in His presence. David, the psalmist, expressed the same sentiment when he wrote: *"How sweet are your words to my taste, sweeter than honey to my mouth!"* (Psalm 119:103 NIV).

Reading the Word is truly delightful when we do it prayerfully and wholeheartedly. The prophet Jeremiah means the same thing when he says: *"When your words came, I ate them; they were my joy and my heart's delight, for I bear your name, O Lord God Almighty."* (Jeremiah 15:16 NIV)

When you know God's Word, it will fill you with joy, power, anointing and the authority of Spirit. The Apostle Peter says to us in his first letter: "Like newborn babies, crave pure spiritual milk, so that by it you may grow up in your salvation" (1 Peter 2:2 NIV).

When we feed daily on the Word, like a baby that craves his mother's milk, the Lord will pour upon us wisdom and understanding. Then we will be able to grow spiritually, mature, be fashioned by the Lord and be called to the ministry.

In our home we have a box that holds five thousand and four hundred biblical questions, we use them to teach the Scriptures to Kathryn and Junior in our spare time. Considering our children's age, for they are still very young, the knowledge they have in God's Word is enormous.

During a children's service, Kathryn sang and Junior preached the Word in front of two hundred and thirty children in the City of Los Angeles. He had already preached to the Sunday school kids of our Assembly of God Church, when he was only five. We know that God has a plan for Kathryn and Josué Yrión, Jr.. And as parents it's our responsibility to teach them the wealth and the eternal treasures of God's Word while they grow so that tomorrow, when they are called to the ministry, they will have a solid base in the knowledge of the Word. We also teach them three languages: English, Spanish, and Portuguese. During a year, they read the Bible in English and Spanish along with my wife Damaris. In the near future, I will read the Bible with them in Portuguese. Feed your children and your family with God's Word. The Bible is the Meal of meals because its spiritual food.

4 — The Inspiring Power of God's Word

"All Scripture is God-breathed and is useful for teaching, rebuking, correcting and training in righteousness."

2 Timothy 3:16 NIV

Being inspired by God, the Bible, through its pages has the power to inspire others. God, not men, inspires it! The Lord revealed to the prophet: *"Take a scroll and write on it all the words I have spoken to you concerning Israel, Judah and all the other nations from the time I began speaking to you in the reign of Josiah till now"* (Jeremiah 3:2 NIV)

God spoke to us since those times, He speaks today, and He will continue to speak tomorrow. The Bible reveals that God always speaks to man.

"In the past God spoke to our forefathers through the prophets at many times and in various ways, but in these last days he has spoken to us by his Son..."

Hebrews 1:1-2 NIV

The Bible declares that God has spoken in many ways. When God delivered Israel out of Egypt, He delivered His people out of bondage by His Word; which speaks of Christ delivering us from our sins. When God opened the Red Sea, He was speaking of His extraordinary power. When we were baptized in Christ' death we resurrected to a new life; we've moved out of death into life. When Joshua conquered the "promised land", it spoke of Christ conquering victory on the cross and rising victoriously from the dead. Through Joshua, God was saying to us that He would give us the promised land of Heaven, which is our spiritual inheritance. When Joshua defeated the king of Jericho and destroyed the walls of the city, God was saying that nothing would be impossible for us in our spiritual walk, if we fix our eyes on Jesus during the times of tribulation and proving. In conclusion, through the pages of the Old Testament, God spoke "many times and in many ways." Let God speak to you through His Word!

In August of 1999, preparing to leave for a crusade where I would be ministering in Madras, India, our children were very concerned for our safety. They were afraid that something dreadful could happen to us. I remember that Pastor Wilmar Silviera and his wife were visiting us at our home, (Pastor Wilmar and his wife are our ministry directors and were also traveling with us) and Kathryn and Junior hugged us weeping in worry. As I watched this scene, my heart was moved to compassion, and I wept with love and affection for our children, I went up the flight of stairs with my family and into the bedroom. There we knelt and prayed to the Lord that He would keep our children as well as Pastor Wilmar and Christina's children, in New Jersey during our trip. Later on in the night, I went to Kathryn's, and Junior's bedroom, smelled their pillows, and wept before God: "Lord, I want to return home with my wife and the Wilmars. I want to see my children again. I want to live! Lord, deliver us from every attack and every sickness and disease that would come against us. You know that many of your servants have died in India because of the Word." I wept much in both of their rooms, and asked the Lord to give me a word. When I opened the Bible, I found God speaking to me through the Book of Joshua: *"No one will be able to stand up against you all the days of your life. As I was with Moses, so I will be with you; I will never leave you nor forsake you… Be strong and very courageous. Have I not commanded you? Be strong and courageous. Do not be terrified; do not be discouraged, for the Lord your God will be with you wherever you go."* (Joshua 1:5,9 NIV)

God spoke to me because I need a word that would bring comfort. I needed to hear that word before I went on to India. God speaks today!

In the Book of the prophet Ezekiel, we read: *"the word of the Lord came to Ezekiel the priest"* (Ezekiel 1:3b NIV) The Word is inspired by God and His Word comes forth from Him. Who wrote the Ten Commandments? God did, with His own finger. God inspired all the Scripture in the Bible; He was who led men into writing it.

Every enacted human law, that is contrary to God's Word, will one day stand trial before Him. All the laws that permit abortion, while the Bible clearly states that God is the avenger of innocent blood, will one day be judged before God. Every part of the laws that protect perverted sexual practices (against what He established as a normal and healthy relationship between one man and one woman, rightfully married) will in deed be judged. In the first chapter of Romans, it says that these peoples' thinking has become futile, foolish, and darkened, because of their perversion. Woe unto the politicians that enacted laws against the Bible, prayer, and Christ' Church! Woe unto the presidents, governors, senators, legislators and congress-people that approve law that are contrary to God ridiculing His Word! They will all stand one day before the Great White Throne. None of them will be able to escape. The Apostle Paul states that God *"has set a day when he will judge the world with justice by the man he has appointed."* (Act 17:31 NIV) They will be judged for violating God's moral, written and spiritual law. All of these laws are in the Bible, His Word! We can become wise through them, be led and be eternally saved. Hallelujah!

> *"Brothers, the Scripture had to be fulfilled which the Holy Spirit spoke long ago through the mouth of David…"*

Acts 1:16a NIV

The Word of God always comes to pass! It's not the word of men but God's Word!

Paul also said: *"The Holy Spirit spoke the truth to your forefathers when he said through Isaiah the prophet…"* (Acts 28:25 NIV)

In the past, the Spirit of God had spoken to the rebellious people of Israel. God speaks many times and in different ways to a generation that is also rebellious and disobedient in our days. It is the Holy Spirit who brings conviction, leads the sinner to repentance, exhorts, speaks, reveals, and brings us to tears.

It doesn't matter how well instructed and learned a preacher may be, how many doctorates have been obtained, how nicely the outlines are prepared, or how convincing the homiletic-hermeneutic rhetoric might sound. If he or she is not filled of the Holy Spirit, the message will be dry and the result will be failure. The Word that we are talking about is not of human conviction, but divine, full of power, extraordinary, and its anointing breaks the devil's yoke. Hallelujah!

If God inspires the Word, and men instructed by the Holy Spirit wrote it (2 Peter 1:21), why are people so full of doubt, unbelief and lack of faith? Let's get back into God Word and get right with Him that we may start to grow again in His Word, loving it, respecting it, and obeying it. Hallelujah!

Brother Andrew, of *"Mision Puertas Abiertas"* (Mission of the Open Doors) also known as "God's smuggler" delivered one million Bibles into China during the 1980's. The ministry's mission was called "The Pearl Project". As soon as the Bibles arrived, there were thousands of Christians waiting to help unload the ship. Many of them saw a man dressed in a white garment that was walking on the beach. The Lord did not allow the Chinese radars to pick up on the ship that carried the Bibles. This is a clear indication that Jesus was there! It was a historical time for the Church breaking into the Communist countries that formed the Bamboo curtain. God triumphed! His Word triumphed! Christ's Church triumphed!

During the time that the Berlin Wall fell at the end of the 1980s, and God delivered the countries of Eastern Europe out of the communist curse of the terrible Iron Curtain, He was saying: "I will build my Church and the gates of hell will not prevail against it!"

On May 7th of 1992, the National Day of Prayer in the United States, my wife, my brother-in-law, Obed, and I were invited together with a group of black, Korean and

Latin American ministers to attend a service at Dr. E.V. Hill's Mt. Zion Missionary Baptist Church, where President George Bush would give a talk. You may have heard about the Rodney King case of Los Angeles, in which he was beaten by local police officers. The story was spread all over the world by the media. After the trials, the police officers were released, and a massive riot of the black community took place. Thousands of houses and buildings in black neighborhoods were burned down along the streets of South Central Los Angeles. George Bush, who was the president at that time, came to L.A. to try to reconcile the black and white communities. During his speech, using a loud voice, looking and pointing at us (the ministers on the platform), said: "The United States needs to return back to God! The answer to racism is not in me or in the government; it's with these ministers. We must return to the Bible, God's Word, and the Lord will help us resolve our differences and end with this destruction that we've seen today, here, in the streets of Los Angeles, California. America needs to return to the principles of love and acceptance in God's Word." In fact, former President Bush was absolutely right! It's toward the Word and the principles of the Scriptures that we need to return.

Dear reader, the Bible has the power to turn your life around completely. If you haven't given your life to Christ yet, do it right now. Let God work in your life, and He will surely help you in all the realms of life.

In this chapter, we've seen how God's Word works. It has the power to influence, to stand, to nourish and to inspire. The Bible has the power to influence my life as well as yours. The Word has the power to stand in our lives forever. It also has the power to nourish our spirit and finally, the Word has the power to inspire us. Believe the Word, live and walk in the Word. Jesus is the Word of God, and Jesus is God's revealed Word to us. "The revelation of Jesus Christ, which God gave him to show his servants what must soon take place. He made it known by sending his angel to his servant John, who testifies to everything he saw—that is, the word of God and the testimony of Jesus Christ. Blessed is the one who reads the words of this prophecy, and blessed are those who hear it and take to heart what is written in it, because the time is near." (Revelation 1:1-3 NIV)

We are very near the end times; our redemption is at hand. The prophecies are being fulfilled very quickly. Jesus is at the point of returning for His Church. Just looking at the Middle East is enough to give us proof that the prophecies about the nation of Israel are being fulfilled to the last detail, just as Christ said. There is no error in God's Word. It's absolute and exact in every prediction. May God be with us! Maranatha!

Chapter Three

What Does The Bible Mean To Us?

*"These commandments that I give you today are to
be upon your hearts. Impress them on your children.
Talk about them when you sit at home and when you
walk along the road, when you lie down and when you get
up. Tie them as symbols on your hands and bind them on
your foreheads."*

Deuteronomy 6:6-9 NIV

Returning home one night from a service in Los
Angeles, I opened the door and my wife, Damaris, immediately signaled to me to hide behind the living room sofa
so that I could hear what our daughter Kathryn was saying to her brother. They were pretending to be in a service
and, if they saw me, they would quit, and all the humor of
it would be lost. Kathryn was standing very close to
Junior with her book: "Mi Primera Biblia" (My First
Bible) in hand. Fixing her eyes on her brother, she
preached to him: "Junior, don't be rebellious like Jonah"
—He's only two years old— He raised his little hand and
replied: "But Kathy, I'm not Jonah, I'm Junior, your
brother. I am Junior, Kathy…" Children… How wonderful to have them with us.

The words of God are words of life. They made the
worlds. When you study them and believe in them, you
will gain their instruction, wisdom and understanding.

They will provide you with the understanding you
need to live a clean, righteous, and holy life before God

and men. Living in line with the Word will take you into the realm of unceasing victory.

The Bible is written in Our Hearts

What does the Bible mean to us? It is the living word that is written inside of us: in our heart, soul, and spirit. It speaks on the inside that as parents we are responsible for teaching biblical principles to our children, in the home, traveling, before bedtime, and starting the day. Its precepts and commandments must always rule in our heart. The Book of Proverbs teaches us the following: "Above all else, guard your heart, for it is the wellspring of life." (Proverbs 4:23 NIV) Dr. Tim LaHaye, referring to the Bible once said: "This Book either separates me from sin, or sin separates me from this Book." The Bible states that sin is in the heart of men. And in the heart is where God's Word must be kept. Speaking of the heart of men, Jesus said: "For from within, out of men's hearts, come evil thoughts, sexual immorality, theft, murder, adultery, greed, malice, deceit, lewdness, envy, slander, arrogance and folly. All these evils come from inside and make a man unclean." (Mark 7:21-23 NIV) It's inside the heart where we must put God's Word.

Sin is fed in the mind, then it goes into the heart, and finally, it leads to an action. Ministers don't commit adultery overnight. It doesn't happen so quickly as it may apparently seem; it's a process. First, they quit praying, fasting, and reading the Word, and when they do read the Word, it's only to prepare a sermon and preach it, not to apply it in their lives. They neglect their personal walk, their family and their spouse. Abandoning prayer, fasting and the Word, they then lose the fear of God. Next, they become insensitive to the voice of God, and that's where the devil steps in to offer sin as something inoffensive to God, as if it were something completely natural. Or maybe, something that's bad, but necessary to do, deceiving them into sinning against God, their spouse, their children, their family, and their Church. Consequently, because of their sin they lose their reputation, their good name, their integrity, their ministry and the anointing. Besides this they also lose e the respect of their family, colleagues and the Church. After conjugal infidelity, the marriage will never be the same again. Minister, guard your life! Brother, sister, guard your life! Youth, flee from fornication! It's not worth it to sin.

I have met many ministry colleagues and other people who have fallen into adultery whose lives are destroyed to this day. And this has even happened to those who have repented of their actions. If you sin, your life will never be the same. Listen to God's voice, don't do it! Run to the foot of the cross, get on your knees and pray; the Holy Spirit will help you to overcome temptation, for it is written: "No temptation has seized you except what is common to man. And God is faithful; he will not let you be tempted beyond what you can bear. (1 Corinthians 10:13 NIV)

In my travels around the world, I must watch constantly, every day. Only God can guard my soul. I endeavor to walk in wisdom and keep God's Word in my heart. The admonition we find in Deuteronomy is unmistakable: "Fix these words of mine in your hearts and minds." (Deuteronomy 11:18b NIV) Here is the secret of spiritual victory! We need to guard and treasure the Word in our heart. It must be written on the inside of us. There is no excuse to not keep His Word. "Now what I am commanding you today is not too difficult for you or beyond your reach. It is not up in heaven, so that you have to ask, 'Who will ascend into heaven to get it and proclaim it to us so we may obey it?' No, the word is very near you; it is in your mouth and in your heart so you may obey it." (Deuteronomy 30:11-14 NIV)

The Word is written in our hearts. There is no reason to sin! In Jesus' Name the victory is ours! On one occasion, David the psalmist said: " I have hidden your word in my heart that I might not sin against you." (Psalm 119:11 NIV) Keep, guard and secure His Word inside your heart forever; it is the only antidote against disobedience and sin. One time a preacher gave a passionate sermon against sin. He preached boldly, daringly and with courage. The Church was packed; it was a Sunday morning service. When the pastor of the congregation heard the message delivered with such passion, heart and courage, he was disgusted, for it was a liberal-oriented Church. Because of his unrest, he approached the courageous speaker and said: "Don't say sin; say natural disorder or psychological disorder, because if you say that everything is a sin people will be offended...Change the way you label things."

The preacher very calmly called someone to sing a hymn and, bringing his message to a standstill, said to the pastor: "I'll be right back!" He ran to the pharmacy, bought a bottle of poison, and ran back to the Church. Resuming his talk, he addressed the pastor and the Church: "In my hands I have a bottle of poison. I'm going to change the name of the poison; I will peel the label off and write children's candy." So he took a pencil, and peeling of the label off, he wrote what he had said he would. He then gave it to the pastor and said: "Now drink it with water!" The pastor leaped from the pew that was on the platform and said: "I can't have this! You changed the label, but the content is still poison." Then the preacher said to the pastor and the Church: "What you want me to do is the same. You want me to change the label, but sin will always be sin. Even if you do change the label, sin will always be sin, the mortal venom of those who disobey and transgress the Word of God." The young preacher was right! You can name things whichever way you want, but sin will always be sin.

In the Gospel of Luke we read that Mary, the mother of Jesus, "treasured all these things in her heart." (Luke 1:51 NIV) Don't keep God's Word only in your head; but treasure it in your heart like Mary did. You may have known the Word in your mind, but if you don't guard it in your heart, sin will destroy you, because you cannot overcome sin with your intellect, but only by the power of the Spirit of God. The Apostle Paul teaches us is Romans: "This is the word of faith we are proclaiming." (Romans 10:8b NIV) Paul understood about the power of the Word in the heart and cited the Scripture in the Book of Deuteronomy. On a different occasion, speaking to the Colossians, Paul warned them as follows: "Let the word of Christ dwell in you richly as you teach and admonish one another with all wisdom, and as you sing psalms, hymns and spiritual songs with gratitude in your hearts to God." (Colossians 3:16 NIV) Let God's Word dwell in your life!

The Bible is Light to our Heart

God's Word ministers light in the darkness of our heart; which is daily attacked by the enemy. The psalmist declares: "The precepts of the Lord are right, giving joy to the heart. The commands of the Lord are radiant, giving light to the eyes." (Psalm 19:8 NIV) The Bible makes us see things that otherwise we wouldn't perceive. It shines in the dark, giving us light and wisdom in difficult issues. The light it radiates gives us the ability to overcome in every realm of life, and it allows us to see those secret things or sins, that are hidden inside the heart.

One time a young girl got lost on a lake while riding in a pedal-boat. It was already dark, and her father went out searching for her with a flashlight. The man yelling would say:

–Baby, say something! Yell so I can hear you!

And she yelled from somewhere in the lake:

–Here I am!

Her father asked her to look at the flashlight and follow the light. That way she would find the river shore. And, directing her path by that light, she found the river shore. When she got there, she jumped out of the pedal boat, and hugging her father, said in relief:

—If it weren't for your voice and the light shining from the flashlight, my friends and I would have been lost on the lake until tomorrow.

The light from the flashlight gave her direction! In the same way, the Bible is a light that leads our path, and the Lord's voice directs us toward the safe shore of our spiritual life. The Bible is light unto our heart. As the psalmist declares: "Your word is a lamp to my feet and a light for my path." (Psalm 119:105 NIV) On one occasion, a sister quoting this Scripture before her congregation, got so nervous that she said the first part of it right, but got confused with the last part and said: "Brethren, the Bible says, Your word is a lamp to my feet… and instead of saying, and a light for my path, she completed the scripture in her own words like this: and…and…and electricity for my path." To that sister, the Bible wasn't only light, but electricity as well. Allow God's electricity, the wonderful light of God's Word fill your heart. The verse of this Scripture in Psalm 119 was one of the first ones that Kathryn and Junior learned. Junior sleeps with his Bible beside his pillow, and sometimes goes to sleep hugging it: that's how much love he has for it. Some days ago, he said that he would take charge of the ministry when I get old. Then I replied: "Junior, that's going to be long ride down the road of life; you will have your calling, your anointing, your gifting, your own ability, and your ministry affiliation without having to walk under my shadow. Study the Word, and one day you will be apt and perfect for every good work." In 1998, I preached in the Luis Aparicio Stadium in Maracaibo, Venezuela. My whole family traveled with me, and after the message, Junior placed his arm around my neck and said: "Daddy, when I grow up I'm going to preach just like you, in a place with lots of people, because I'm learning with you." Junior's words filled my heart with joy and, putting my arm around him, I said: "That's the way it'll be my son. That's the way it'll be in Jesus Name!" Glory to God! Teach your children God's Word by example. Kathryn and Junior have my wife's example and mine. Are you an example to your children? Since they were born our kids play church in our living room. Junior uses a chair as a pulpit placing his Bible on it, and preaches to Kathryn until she is tired of it. A few days ago, Kathryn said to Junior: "Make up some other sermons because I already know these."

Psalm 119 proclaims: "The unfolding of your words gives light; it gives understanding to the simple." (v. 130 NIV) The word gives us understanding, wisdom and light. The Book of Proverbs declares: "For these commands are a lamp, this teaching is a light, and the corrections of discipline are the way to life." (Proverbs 6:23 NIV)

The Word disciplines us by correcting us and giving us light through its commandments. Never flee from God when He corrects you for your wrongdoings. The Word exhorts, corrects, and heals our heart.

Here's what Peter teaches us in his second letter: "And we have the word of the prophets made more certain, and you will do well to pay attention to it, as to a light shining in a dark place, until the day dawns and the morning star rises in your hearts." (2 Peter 1:19 NIV) D.L. Moody said that the Bible is a powerful effective torch.

There was a pilot that was unable to land his small plane because the runway lights were not working. When he called the control tower of the small airport, he told them that he couldn't see the runway to land the plane. Then one of the airport managers got into his car, turned the high beams on, and drove up and down the runway from one end to the other, in such a way that the pilot would be able to see the reflection of light on the runway, and land the aircraft. The pilot, with the help of the car's high beams, was able to land carefully on the runway without any problems. Likewise, the Bible is a light that helps us land our "little airplane" in life, and make the right decisions in the midst of dangerous situations, delivering us out of a crisis.

God's People love the Bible with all their Heart

"For I delight in your commands, which I love, and I meditate on your decrees."

Psalm 119:47 NIV

Do you love God's Word? Is it in the center of your life? What are your daily priorities? Do you spend time studying the Scriptures? If you don't love God's Word, you don't love Jesus because Jesus is the Word of God. Look at what Psalm 119:72 says: *"The law from your mouth is more precious to me than thousands of pieces of silver and gold."* (NIV)

Do you love the Word more than the treasures of this world? If you were to choose between money and the Word, what would be more important in your life? Who is number one in your life? Jesus said in the Gospel of Matthew: "Do not store up for yourselves treasures on earth, where moth and rust destroy, and where thieves break in and steal. But store up for yourselves treasures in heaven, where moth and rust do not destroy, and where thieves do not break in and steal. *For where your treasure is, there your heart will be also."* Matthew 6:19-21 NIV.

What is your priority in life? Becoming rich and powerful? Enjoying earthly pleasures? David the psalmist said: *"Oh, how I love your law! I meditate on it all day long."* Psalm 119:97 NIV. Do you meditate on the Word during the day? Do you take time out to read the Scriptures? Further in this same psalm David goes on to declare: *"Your promises have been thoroughly tested, and your servant loves them.* Psalm 119:140 NIV. Are you expecting something from God? What is your faith founded on? Has He responded to you? Do you believe in His promises?

Voltaire, the rebellious French philosopher, was an atheist. On a certain occasion he was mocking Christianity and said: "One hundred years after my death there will be no more Christians, no more Bibles, no more God's Word; all the memory of these, including Christ and His teachings will disappear." What an irony! One hundred years after Voltaire's death, the French, moved by a deep love for God's Word, used the same print shop and the same machines that Voltaire used to propagate atheism, and printed one million New Testaments on the centennial day of his death... God triumphed! Not even the ashes of Voltaire's bones were around; but God's Word remains forever in our hearts. No one can destroy His Word; it is invincible and indestructible.

I thank God, and always will, for having parents that took me to the Assembly of God Churches in Santa Maria, Rio Grande do Sul, Brazil, to hear the Word of God. On Sunday mornings we would go to Sunday school classes held at the downtown location. In the afternoon, we would go to a small annex in Vila Oliveira for the three o'clock service and then return for the main 7:00 p.m. service held at the downtown Church. In those days, it was a pleasure to hear the Word of God from the lips of my beloved pastor Orvalino Lemos, who is now resting in Christ's eternal mansions. I also thank God because there were men like the beloved pastor Eliseu Dornelles Alves, who guided me in the Word since my youth, and believed in my calling to world missions. Later on, at YWAM (Youth With A Mission), in Bello Horizonte, Minas Gerais, under the leadership of the National Director, Pastor Jim Stier, and the base directors, Pastor Jaime Araujo and his wife Maristela, God molded, discipled and broke my life preparing me for the ministry. Later on, in Madrid, Spain, as a YWAM missionary under pastor Alfonso Cherene's leadership, God continued to work in my life while submitting to the wisdom of the man of God and, proving my call, he launched me to reach the nations. Nowadays, we hold hundreds of evangelistic crusades around the world. To this day, I have preached in seventy countries of every continent. All Glory and Honor belongs to the Lord. I'm eternally grateful to those people who invested their lives in my spiritual formation, feeding me God's Word from childhood on... I received the influence of my parents, then my spiritual leaders, all the way to where I stand today, feeding on His blessed and powerful Word, the Bible, which I love with all of my heart. Hallelujah! Our ministry has reached—by way of audio and videotape—one hundred and twelve countries, in which thousands of people have been born-again, restored, healed, filled with the Holy Spirit, and called to the holy ministry of preaching God's Word. All this is because of Christ, who, through His Word, has made real all of these marvelous projects. To Him be the honor, the glory, the power and praise for ever more. Today, we are reaching nations that were locked up for the Gospel. Recently, I received a letter of invitation for a crusade in Katmandu, Nepal, for a gathering of fifty thousand people. Local pastors are praying and endeavoring to obtain Nepal's official government permits to hold a crusade that will be historic. The people in those places love the Word and many of them have given their lives for the Gospel's sake. Others are locked up in prison cells and tortured for being caught evangelizing on the streets and preaching God's Word, which is still forbidden in the most Muslim, Buddhist and Hindu countries. However, God's Word continues to be loved by His people living in those countries that are extremely closed to the Gospel. Remember that borders do not limit God nor does he need a passport. There are no locked doors for Him; His vocabulary does not include the word "impossible." God has no problems, but rather the solutions to the problems.

The Bible is a great blessing to our heart

The Lord said to Joshua: *"Do not let this Book of the Law depart from your mouth; meditate on it day and night, so that you may be careful to do everything written in it. Then you will be prosperous and successful."* (Joshua 1:8 NIV)

For those who reverence the Scripture and submit to it, there is a great blessing and many promises of prosperity in every realm of life. The Word declares "success" in what we do. David speaking of the precepts and commandments of God's law declares: *"By them is your servant warned; in keeping them there is great reward."* (Psalm 19:11 NIV) If we remain in the Word, we will be rewarded with health, spiritual and financial blessings, and we will enjoy eternal life when He returns for us.

One time, a pastor was preaching about the rapture of the Church. It was a Sunday evening, and the Church was filled to capacity because of the many visitors that were invited for that special meeting. Many unsaved people were there. Culminating the anointed message on Christ's return, the pastor asked how many people would like to be raptured marvelously up to heaven. Many stood up. In the crowd there was a drunkard that had been invited by the Church's doorkeeper and was sitting in the first row of seats, and the pastor asked him: "Friend, wouldn't you like to go up in the rapture? The drunkard got up, looked at the pastor, and said: "Yes, I would like to! But I'm taking the second trip, because the first one is already full." As funny as this incident is, the subject is very serious. There won't be a second trip. You leave on the first one, or you won't leave at all and, will instead be lost forever.

The Bible is a blessing to our hearts, for it tells us that Jesus is coming back. In the first letter of Thessalonians, Paul exhorts us: *"For the Lord himself will come down from heaven, with a loud command, with the voice of the archangel and with the trumpet call of God, and the dead in Christ will rise first. After that, we who are still alive and are left will be caught up together with them in the clouds to meet the Lord in the air. And so we will be with the Lord forever."* (1 Thessalonians 4:16-17 NIV) We will be there! We will see Him just as He is! And everything will be over.

Now, in order for us to reach our celestial mansion of delights with Him, the Lord left us the Bible. His return is a promise for those who reverence the Scriptures. Look at this wonderful blessing: *"Therefore everyone who hears these words of mine and puts them into practice is like a wise man who built his house on the rock. The rain came down, the streams rose, and the winds blew and beat against that house; yet it did not fall, because it had its foundation on the rock."* (Matthew 7:24-25 NIV) These words are for those who have been prudent, wise, and kept the Word. Jesus is the Rock! Testing can come our way, heavy rains can pour, and our lives may be filled with trials and persecutions, the winds of crisis and adversities may blow even to the point of being tortured for His name. All these things can beat against our spiritual life, but our house will not fall, for it's built on the solid Rock, which is Jesus Christ. Hallelujah!

Recently, after preaching my message at a pastors conference in Worcester, Massachusetts, one of the pastors asked to speak with me. He confessed, with tears in his eyes, that a few months earlier he was on the verge of quitting the ministry. He felt too tired and worn-out. Someone lent him a video with a message that I preached about the need to pay the price of discipleship and self-denial. The word encouraged him greatly and lifted his spirit. And getting on his knees, he laid all his burdens on the Lord, and God gave him a new vision. As a result, the

pastor did not quit the ministry but instead was strength-
ened, freshly anointed by the Holy Spirit, and received
power anew to continue with his ministry. God's Word has
power to turn things around! He positioned himself on the
Rock, Jesus Christ. His ministry problems had gone
beyond what he was able to bear. The devil was beating
against this man with all his strength to destroy his spiritual and ministerial house. But the Lord arrived on time as
always. He will never leave you! Never! On the other
hand, God also warns and admonishes us, teaching us
about the consequences for those who don't keep His
Word and don't obey the Scriptures. *"But everyone who hears
these words of mine and does not put them into practice is like a
foolish man who built his house on sand. The rain came down, the
streams rose, and the winds blew and beat against that house, and
it fell with a great crash."* (Matthew 7:26-27 NIV) This is the
portrait of a foolish and thoughtless person. He builds his
house on the sands of the worlds deception, of unwise
riches and pleasures, and on everything this life has to
offer to satisfy the lusts of the flesh. In the ministry realm,
many people have built their house on the sands of intellectual self-importance, arrogance, personal agenda, ego-
tistical fame, popularity and the need to be acknowledged
and applauded by men. Others have built over pride and
the desire to be greater than their colleagues. Many of
these people, after being at the top, shining like stars, hear
the words of Christ: "Great was your fall." May God deliver us from this! Let's pray that you and I would always be
willing to humble ourselves, understanding that we are
nothing without Him. I plead the Blood of Jesus to cover
us!

Great ministries have fallen, causing scandals and dis-
honor to Christ's cause. Build your spiritual and ministeri-

al house on the Eternal Rock, Jesus Christ. Jesus has also left us another invaluable teaching. Let's read what Luke, the evangelist, wrote in his book: "As Jesus was saying these things, a woman in the crowd called out, *"Blessed is the mother who gave you birth and nursed you. He replied, 'blessed rather are those who hear the word of God and obey it'"* (Luke 11:27-28 NIV). Here is the secret. Hear and obey the Word of God. James also exhorts us to not only be hearers: *"Do not merely listen to the word, and so deceive yourselves. Do what it says."* (James 1:22 NIV) This is the key to victory and eternal life! Do the Word, and not merely just listen; treasure it in your heart and keep it forever. Christ Himself, speaking of His Word said: *"I tell you the truth, whoever hears my word and believes him who sent me has eternal life and will not be condemned; he has crossed over from death to life"* (John 5:24 NIV). What a blessing is God's Word in our heart! We have crossed over from death to life, being saved and reconciled by His Word. Lets further read what He goes on to say: "To the Jews who had believed him, Jesus said, *"If you hold to my teaching, your are really my disciples"* (John 8:31 NIV). Discipleship is to know, obey, live and walk in the Word. And reverencing is to respect, give due honor, and regard with esteem and appreciation. During a crusade in April, 1996 in Viña del Mar, Chile, the Lord gave me the honor of being greeted by the Chilean government in the Congress of the Republic, where they granted to me the Congressional Bronze Medal. Later on, they invited me to a different ceremony at the government's "Palacio de Bellas Artes" (The Palace of Beautiful Arts) as "The Son and Illustrious Visitor to Viña del Mar and the Chilean nation." I wrote in the Book of Gold at the government headquarters in Viña del Mar, that I dedicated such privilege and honor in first place to the Lord Jesus

Christ, then to the pastors of the evangelical Churches of Chile, to the President of Chile, its ministers, and to the people of Chile. Everything I had received I dedicated it to them. God honored me on that occasion because I honored Him for so many years. Truly, the Honor is for Him. I am only fulfilling my mission to preach the Good News around the world. I continue to be an unworthy servant as He says in His Word, nothing else. Here's what I am: a simple preacher of the Gospel, like all my colleagues. The Bible is a great blessing to our heart.

The Bible purifies our Heart

Young people come and ask us how can they live a upright life and have integrity before the Lord. The Word of God has a clear answer to this question: *"How can a young man keep his way pure? By living according to your word"* (Psalm 119:9 NIV). If the youth stays in the Word and lives according to it, every realm in their lives will be sanctified and purified. It's God's Word that produces conviction to the youth and leads them into a victorious spiritual life. If you are living in your youth years, guard your heart, pray, fast and study the Word, and God will honor you in due time. Pay the price! T.L Osborn said, "God will use you in the measure you commit yourself to Him." I would say that the more you commit to Him, the more He will use you.

Guard your body, soul, and spirit, and God will use you in great measure. Sanctify your thoughts and your walk, and you will see the wonders God will do in your life. Hallelujah!

About holiness, this is what the Lord says to us: *"You are already clean because of the word I have spoken to you"* (John 15:3 NIV). It's the Word that sanctifies us! The more we read the Bible, the more holy the realms of our life become. If we obey God's Word, we will obtain His approval in everything we do. Listening to the Word of truth and being transformed by the truth, will purify our lives: *"Sanctify them by the truth; your word is truth"* (John 17:17 NIV).

Buddha, at the end of his life declared: "What is truth?" Mohamed, in his last days stated: "I still haven't found the truth!" But Jesus said: *"I am the way and the truth and the life. No one comes to the Father except through me."* (John 14:6 NIV) He is the absolute truth, there is no other! The Word is the truth, and Jesus is the truth because He is the Word.

Concerning the Church, the Bible shows us that: *"...Christ loved the Church and gave himself up for her to make her holy, cleansing hear by the washing with water through the word"* (Ephesians 5:25-26 NIV). We are sanctified and purified by the Word as a holy Church, without blemish, immaculate and irreproachable.

Peter in his second epistle writes to the Church: *"Now that you have purified yourselves by obeying the truth so that you have sincere love for your brothers, love one another deeply, from the heart. For you have been born again, not of perishable seed, but of imperishable, through the living and enduring word of God"* (1 Peter 22-23 NIV). What an extraordinary Scripture! As a Church, we must purify our lives, sanctifying them by the Word. To my fellow ministers, I would say that God uses us and will use us according to the measure of our daily sanctification. Jonathan Edwards, the great preacher of New England said that, "a holy man is a powerful weapon in God's hands." Why are there so many pastors and evangelists on the face of the earth today that have little or no impact with their ministries? Why are there so many churches scattered around the globe with so little influence in our world? If we would examine the lives of these pastors, evangelists, and ministers, we would learn that part of their lives are not upright, holy or pure. Sometimes people say: "Brother Yrión, how is it that God has been able to use you around the world being so young?" Then I reply: "Pay the price that I pay, and God will use you in the same way." This is the right answer. The more you empty yourself, the more He will fill you with His power. The more you die to your flesh, the more life in the Holy Spirit He will give you. The more you die to yourself, your ego, the more He will give you life, humility, character and anointing. The more you submit to His authority, the more he will lift you up and use you in a great and powerful way. And you will serve Him to the end of your life or until the day that He comes to take you away. Hear the Word and obey it!

Many years ago, a great man of God who smuggled Bibles behind the Iron and Bamboo curtains, the communist countries of Eastern Europe and Asia, said to his wife: "I'll be back soon!" Pregnant with their first son, she asked, "Where are you going this time?" He replied: "I'm going to China, North Korea and Burma. I'll be back soon." He kissed his wife and caressing her womb said: "Be good my son, I'll be back!" What this great man of God didn't know is that he would never return to his home again in the US. He went to China, and everything went well. Then to North Korea, and all went well. But on his way to Burma he encountered problems. He was taking a shipment of Bibles to distribute them in some churches, when the communist police at the border stopped him. They took him to a storage tower in the middle of the country; then tied him to the hoist rope, and lifted him up.

They put hooks in his mouth that ripped through his skin and came out through his nostrils. They hanged him by the feet, and place a bucket beneath him so that the blood would drip into the bucket. They broke three bamboo rods on his back. The beating was so brutal that his spine broke through the skin. They plucked his eyes out, broke his teeth and drilled his ears. The communist police were questioning him to obtain the pastors' whereabouts, so that they could execute them; but he did not respond to them, and they tortured him.

In spite of the terrible torture and suffering death, he was tortured for loving Jesus and smuggling Bibles. He died for the Lord's sake without backing down or denying Him. He died as a true man of God. His crime was taking God's Word to those who didn't have it. When his wife received the telegram that described what was done to him, she had a shock so great that the child turned in her womb, chocking himself with the umbilical chord. What a tragedy! Two lives had now gone, father and son, the latter before he was born, and the father, for the love of God's Word. O God...

While many are willing to give their lives to take God's Word to the desperate, many others that have the Word, are not interested in it. This brother died bravely on the battle line, as a man, even as a man of God. He died for the sake of God's Word, that it would be preached in the lesser-evangelized countries of the 10/40 window, in Burma. While we have the opportunity to have a thousand Bibles, there are millions of other souls longing and praying to have at least one copy of it.

God welcomed this man that was ready and prepared to come into his Heavenly home. This brave and holy man fulfilled his calling. And, purified by the Word, he was able to say: *"For I am already being poured out like a drink offer-ing, and the time has come for my departure. I have fought the good fight, I have finished the race, I have kept the faith. Now there is in store for me the crown of righteousness, which the Lord, the right-eous Judge, will award to me on that day – and not only to me, but also to all who have longed for His appearing"* (2 Timothy 4:6-8 NIV). Paul, a great man of God, was decapitated for lov-ing the Word. The Bible smuggler of Burma was also tor-tured and died for loving the Word. As you read, there are other great men and women sacrificing their lives for the sake of the Word. And as we remain faithful to Him, we will also come into eternal life, in the midst of whatever the circumstances, in sacrifice or torture, free or imprisoned, satisfied or hungry, cold or warm. Be it day or night, in any place, nation, or land: Are you ready to place your life on the line so that others can receive what you have received through the Word of God? Let's pray that God helps us to be faithful and treasure the Word in our heart. Treasure His Word in your life, and God will treasure you! It is a great blessing!

Chapter Four

The Bible – Written With a Purpose

"Jesus did many other miraculous signs in the presence of his disciples, which are not recorded in this book"

(John 20:30 NIV).

When coming back from a trip I always like to bring back gifts for Kathryn and Junior. This has been a habit since they were born. Be it international or domestic travel, I never fail to buy them a gift of some kind. Last year, while preparing my trip to France and Belgium for a series of evangelistic events and meetings in Great Britain, Kathryn sat down on the stairway and began to cry. Then hugging me she said: "Daddy, I don't want you to go, I love you very much and I'm going to miss you…" Junior was standing beside her, too, apparently not paying much attention. Nevertheless, he hugged me and kissed me too. Kathryn continued hugging me tight and crying for some time. Then, Junior, watching his sister insisting that I not leave on this trip, looked at her, and shaking his head 'no', he said: "Kathy, don't ask Daddy not to go on his trip because if he doesn't go he won't bring us any gifts…" Kids are really smart, don't you think ?

The Bible and Its Purpose for our Lives

For what reason has God left us with this Book? What was His purpose in leaving us the Scriptures? Why is the Bible so important for us? It is called the Book of all books. In regard to this we read: *"For you have exalted above all things your name and your word"* (Psalm 138:2b NIV).

What is that, which the Lord exalted, made great, excellent and powerful? His Name and His Word! There is no name under the heavens, in high places or beneath the earth, or the whole universe that can compare to the Name of the Lord and the power of His Word, the Bible. Hallelujah!

> *"My name will be great among the nations, from the rising to the setting of the sun... For I am a great king", says the Lord Almighty.*

> Malachi 1:11a,14b NIV

The first president of the United States, referring to God's Word and to the nations, once said: "It's impossible to rule the world without God and the Bible". He was absolutely right! America was founded on biblical principles and the fear of God. The American Constitution was established on God's Word, and this is why it became a prosperous, powerful and just nation in its laws. Unfortunately, today it's no longer as it was. Politicians have abandoned God's law and have compromised under secular pressures, which are lewd and worldly, in opposition to what God established in the Holy Scriptures. Former President Bill Clinton based his administration on dishonesty, lies, and scandalous immorality. He was a man with charisma but with a serious lack of a solid Christian character, supporting liberal groups that uphold immorality, perversion and corruption as a way of life. In addition, his administration supported groups in favor of abortion. Systematically, the blood of innocent aborted children is being offered upon the altar of holocaust to Molech, the god of blood. These children can't even plead their defense because these women believe they are defending their rights, while the human beings in their wombs are pulled out and squashed into pieces by a cruel surgical instrument, murdered before they can ever say a word.

The Bible is very clear where it says: *"Blessed is the nation whose God is the Lord, the people he chose for his inheritance"* (Psalm 33:12 NIV).

For this purpose, God has left us His Word: So that nations may be guided by Him, that they would fear Him and walk in His ways, obeying His Laws and Precepts, which are based in righteousness, in mutual respect, and in social justice; that everyone can enjoy an abundant life, speaking of our earthly needs, and inherit eternal life in Christ Jesus, our Lord.

1 — The Bible was written for a special purpose

The Bible was written with the purpose of authenticating Christ's Divinity, his divine and celestial nature.

The Gospel of John declares: *"But these are written that you may believe that Jesus is the Christ, the Son of God, and that by believing you may have life in his name"* (John 20:31 NIV). The signs that Christ manifested were written that we would believe in His Word and receive life in His Name. As I mentioned before, His Name is exalted above every nation and there is none comparable to Him. It's only in His name that we can receive forgiveness of sin. Luke declares: *"Salvation is found in no one else, for there is no other name under heaven given to men by which we must be saved"* (Acts 4:12 NIV). That name is Jesus Christ! There is no other! For this reason, the apostles, even in their prisons, "were full of the Holy Spirit, and spoke God's Word with boldness." The Bible was written with the purpose of leading us into eternal life, and that we could walk in his wisdom to obtain a so great salvation through Jesus Christ, our Lord and Savior.

The Bible was written to give us testimony of the truth. *"This is the disciple who testifies to these things and who wrote them down. We know that his testimony is true"* (John 21:24 NIV).

The purpose that God had in leaving us Christ's Words and His deeds is to lead into the truth that we may live by it. John tells us that during Christ's ministry on earth, *"He did many other things…if every one of them were written down…even the whole world would not have room for the books that would be written"* (John 21:25 NIV). Can you understand the greatness of Christ' works? Can you imagine the power in His words and in the miracles, while great multitudes come out to hear Him? It's awesome! Reading the Scriptures, we seldom stop to meditate upon this verse. And it's of vital importance because it reveals that God was interested enough to leave us an inspired, divine, and eternal book that we could know Him. In all He did, Jesus was the accurate divine reproduction of the Heavenly Father's Words and deeds. To know God, you must first know Christ, you must know the Word, and the Word is Christ… Hallelujah! Jesus reflected His Father in all of His deeds and thoughts. The fullness of the Father was in the Son. Let's read what Paul said: *"For God was pleased to have all his fullness dwell in him"* (Colossians 1:19 NIV). Further on, in the same epistle Paul declares: *"For in Christ all the fullness of the Deity lives in bodily form"* (Colossians 2:9 NIV). The Scriptures were left to us that we could understand the fullness of the Son.

The Bible was also written to teach us to live under the principle of hope. *"For everything that was written in the past was written to teach us, so that through endurance and the encouragement of the Scriptures we might have hope"* (Romans 15:4 NIV). In the light of God's Word, have faith, patience and hope. You must continuously believe in the power of God's Word, and fix your daily hopes in the Scriptures. Believe that your spouse and your family will be saved. Set your hopes in God's Word and believe in the power of His Word.

For a long time, a sister in Christ prayed for her son who was unsaved. She would always pray behind a curtain in a corner of her living room. Her house was small and very humble. She spent countless hours fasting and praying for her son. One day, very early in the morning, her son returned home from an all night party with his friends, at that same time the mother was praying and said to her son: "Son, you will never go so far that my prayers can't reach you..." Time went by, and this sister passed away not seeing her rebellious and disobedient son turn back to God. However, one day, after his mother's death, some people came to buy their house, which they had put up for sale. In showing them the house, they came to a corner of the living room, and pulling up the curtain he saw how the wooden floors had worn out where she use to kneel down to pray, and her tears had left visible signs on the old rugged floors. Immediately, the Holy Spirit had him remember his mother's words: "Son, you will never go so far that my prayers can't reach you..." When those words resounded in his heart, he was convicted by the Holy Ghost. Without much explanation to the people who were with him, he fell to the floor in tears trying to recollect with his hands the loving tears with which his mother had saturated the old wooden floor; tears which where poured out because of the suffering he had caused. He cried with a loud voice: "Mother, mother, my dear mama, where are you? I want to see you again some day. I want Christ! I want Jesus! Oh Lord, have mercy on me, save my soul for which my mother prayed so fervently. I give my heart to you, oh God..." Hallelujah!

This young man came back to God because of perseverance, patience, hope, and faith that his mother had in the Scriptures. Although she did not see this much awaited event in this life, she will see her son happy in Jesus in eternity. Realize, that the tears you have shed in prayer, with your faith placed on the Word of God, will never be in vain. Everything is before the presence of God Almighty. You just need to trust His Word, and He will do what He promised: *"Believe in the Lord Jesus, and you will be saved—you and your household"* (Acts 16:31 NIV).

Dear reader, you could be facing the same family situation. Or maybe you're just praying for a friend or acquaintance. Keep praying for them! Only believe the Word of God, and He will give you the victory, no matter what your challenge is.

For our example

One of the reasons the Bible was written was to give us examples and warnings of other people's experiences that we may learn through them. *"These things happened to them as examples and were written down as warnings for us"* (1 Corinthians 10:11 NIV). We must not repeat the same errors of those who stumbled in the Scriptures, but rather practice the right things that they did; for their accounts are recorded in the pages of the Holy Bible for us as an admonition to all of us.

The adulteries, disobediences and unfaithfulness to the Lord and His Word, as well as the heroic deeds of the mentioned saints, were recorded for the purpose of serving as warnings and examples to edify our lives. The epistle to the Hebrews declares: *"Remember your leaders, who spoke the word of God to you. Consider the outcome of their way of life and imitate their faith"* (Hebrews 13:7 NIV). During my lifetime I have learned from many men of God that were and are an example to me in their private, public, and spiritual lives. As a result of this, other men have said that I've been an example to their lives and ministries. Some of them have learned from our faithfulness to God and His Word. It's a great responsibility to model ministry to others.

Knowledge of Eternal Life

The Scriptures were also written to give us knowledge of eternal life in Christ Jesus: *"I write these things to you who believe in the name of the Son of God so that you may know that you have eternal life"* (1 John 5:13 NIV). Furthermore, John declares: *"We know also that the Son of God has come and has given us understanding, so that we may know him who is true. And we are in him who is true—even in his Son Jesus Christ. He is the true God and eternal life"* (1 John 5:20 NIV). Buddha, at the end of his life said: "I haven't yet found the truth!" Mohammad, at the end of his life declared: "What is truth?" However, Jesus said: *"I am the way and the truth and the life"* (John 14:6a NIV). Christ spoke to us about a way; He is the way! Christ spoke to us about truth; He is the truth! Christ spoke to us about life; He is the life! All other religions are false. They're full of false gods, and they are all cults! All other ways or paths, except those indicated by God's Word are false. This is not arrogance or self-importance on my part, but an actual, genuine and truthful fact. Jesus Christ is the absolute truth. Everything else is error, falsehood, deceit and lies. Who says this? Me?

NO! The Bible, the only final authority on spiritual matters, gives to men that they may know the only true God, the Lord Jesus Christ.

Glory to God for His wonderful Word!

2 — The Bible was written with the purpose of being read in the congregation.

The Bible declares in the book of Exodus that Moses *"took the Book of the Covenant and read it to the people. They responded, 'we will do everything the Lord has said; we will obey'"* (Exodus 24:7 NIV).

Joshua did the same thing when he stepped up to take Moses' place: *"Afterward, Joshua read all the words of the law — the blessings and the curses —just as it is written in the Book of the Law"* (Joshua 8:34 NIV). When the Word is read and preached in public in the pulpits of our congregations, the people of God learn to fear and reverence the teaching of the Holy Book. God ordained Moses and Joshua to do it for a basic reason and purpose. Let's read what Deuteronomy states in chapter six: *"The Lord commanded us to obey all these decrees and to fear the Lord our God, so that we might always prosper and be kept alive, as is the case today. And if we are careful to obey all this law before the Lord our God, as he has commanded us, that will be our righteousness"* (Deuteronomy 6:24-25 NIV). When we hear the Word, we must obey, for it is our guarantee that all things will go well. Joshua read the word and obeyed: *"There was not a word of all that Moses had commanded that Joshua did not read to the whole assembly of Israel"* (Joshua 8:35 NIV).

One time a pastor went to Kiev, Ukraine, to preach the Word after it had been freed from the yoke communism. He took a box with him with about one hundred Bibles to give away to those who would go to hear him speak. As soon as he arrived, to his surprise, there was a gathering of thirty to thirty-five thousand people to hear the Word of God. Seeing the multitude, the pastor asked the Lord: "God, how am I to distribute 100 Bibles among all these people?" To which the Lord replied: "This people hunger and thirst after me. This is what you will do: first, you will preach the Word publicly. Then you will pull out every page of every gospel, out of each of the Bibles that you brought, and have the people form a line and you will hand to each person a page of the Bible because one page of my Word is enough to feed them spiritually and take them into eternal life" Wow that's the power of the Word of God! Just one page is enough to satiate someone and lead him or her into the knowledge of Christ. Oh that we may read, preach and obey God's Word.

The Bible declares in the Book of the prophet Jeremiah that *"Baruch son of Neriah did everything Jeremiah the prophet told him to do; at the Lord's temple he read the words of the Lord from the scroll"* (Jeremiah 36:8 NIV). When we hear the words written in the Bible at the Lord's temple, we are instructed, taught and trained in the Holy ways of the Lord. Solomon wrote in Ecclesiastes: *"The words of the wise are as goads, and as nails fastened by the master of assemblies, which are given from one shepherd"* (Ecclesiastes 12:11 KJV). The Bible was written to be read in the congregation of Israel and in the Church of our days. When a pastor preaches the Word, he is teaching out of a book whose wisdom will never fade. For centuries preachers have proclaimed these words in thousands upon thousands of sermons, but always out of the same verses. Everyone prepares his or her own sermon, according to the revelation that God gives each one. The Holy Spirit is the one who gives the emphasis and the application according to what the congregation needs. There are thousands of preachers that prepare thousands of sermons that are heard by millions of people around the world, but God's Word is the same. Every Sunday, the Bible is read publicly in thousands of pulpits; the same Book with the same verses, but ministered in thousands of different ways, one differing from the other, by thousands of different preachers in every nation on the face of the earth, in innumerable languages and dialects, to thousands of singular cultures. This is where the secret of God's wonderful Word resides. The Bible is not a book written by the will of man, but divine, as we've seen before. There is no other book capable of producing the results of the Bible.

Jesus himself emphasized the reading of the Scriptures. Let's read Luke 4:16-17: *"He went to Nazareth, where he had been brought up, and on the Sabbath day he went into the synagogue, as was his custom. And he stood up to read. The scroll of the prophet Isaiah was handed to him. Unrolling it, he found the place where it is written"*.

Jesus understood the importance of reading God's Word publicly. He found the place where it spoke of him. It was the fulfillment of the Scriptures. They never fail. The apostle Paul was also very emphatic affirming the importance of the public reading of the Scriptures when he wrote to the Colossians: *"After this letter has been read to you, see that it is also read in the church of the Laodiceans and that you in turn read the letter from Laodicea"* (Colossians 4:16 NIV). Paul believed it to be very important that the Churches read publicly the letters that he wrote. This was the purpose for his letters; that they be read, obeyed and followed through a radical, complete, and truthful discipleship program.

Queen Elizabeth of England once said: "The Bible and its lectures are the reason for British excellence." Hallelujah! The world leaders of the past recognized that absolute authority of the Bible, its place of prominence, and its purpose for every realm of life.

3 — The Bible was written to be a norm for rule and faith.

The world cannot be ruled without norms that decide right from wrong, which defines what's moral from immoral, or a truth from a lie. When you are driving and arrive to an intersection where a police officer is present, directing traffic with his hands, undoubtedly you will stop at his command. Why? Because the uniform he is wearing represents the authority and the power that the state has vested in him. An officer has the earthly authority to do what he does because the law has conferred those powers upon him. In the same manner, the Bible has the authority and the divine power that God has given it, to guide our life in agreement with that which is written. All we need to do is stand on the Word and say to the world that the Bible was written to be the foundation of our faith, the norms and rule for our conduct, practice and behavior.

The word *"norm"* derives of the Greek word *"gnorisma"*, which means a sign, a mark, a recognizable measure. Ethically, a moral norm should adjust our deeds and behaviors. Now let's look at the meaning of the word *"conduct"*. In general, ethics is the science of behavior. Conduct is a constant attitude (a series of conscious deeds) with a final purpose. Therefore, ethics is a code of rules; the moral principles that rule our conduct and by which we consider other people's behavior; it is the reference point for discerning right and wrong Hence, ethics is the science of norms, because it searches for a norm by which it can set rules and laws of conduct. So therefore, an ethical conduct is simply a conduct in accordance with certain norms or rules that are established with the purpose to be obeyed, to display a clean, impeccable and mature behavior. Pirk Aboth said, "There are three crowns: the crown of wisdom, the crown of priesthood, and the crown of royalty. However, the crown of good reputation and of blameless behavior exceeds them all."

The Bible states the rules for our faith and conduct

The Book of Proverbs declares: *"Where there is no revelation, the people cast off restraint; but blessed is he who keeps the law"* (Proverbs 29:18 NIV). If there's no teaching of the Word, the people have no direction; and if we don't obey the law, the divine and the earthly, we fall into transgression of that which was established spiritually and for this life. Isaiah declares: *"To the law and to the testimony! If they do not speak according to this word, they have no light of dawn"* (Isaiah 8:20 NIV). What was written was written for us. If we don't obey the Bible as our rule of faith and norm of conduct, we will never see the light of dawn, so to speak, we will have no future, and we won't be blessed nor prospered, spiritually or in this life. One thing is attached to the other. Jesus said in the Gospel of Matthew: *"I tell you the truth, whatever you bind on earth will be bound in heaven, and whatever you loose on earth will be loosed in heaven"* (Matthew 18:18 NIV). There is no other way! What God has established, is decreed! We need to obey the rules, norms and laws that God established in nature. The laws of physics cannot be altered. And we also need to obey the Word of God, the spiritual Law. It's very simple. In the Gospel of

John Jesus said: *"There is a judge for the one who rejects me and does not accept my words; that very word which I spoke will condemn him at the last day"* (John 12:48 NIV). To obey or not to obey is a matter of free will, option, election or decision. He who hears the Word of God and obeys it has already received his reward and will also receive life eternal. He that refuses to obey God's Word has already received his "reward" through a life of defeat, sickness and destruction, and will receive the punishment of eternal affliction. *"God is just: He will pay back trouble to those who trouble you and give relief to you who are troubled, and to us as well. This will happen when the Lord Jesus is revealed from heaven in blazing fire with his powerful angels. He will punish those who do not know God and do not obey the gospel of our Lord Jesus. They will be punished with everlasting destruction and shut out from the presence of the Lord and from the majesty of his power..."* (2 Thessalonians 1:6-9 NIV). This is the message: Obedience or Disobedience. Heaven or Hell. Make haste! This is the final word.

Let's recall the Apostle Paul's exhortation: *"But even if we or an angel from heaven should preach a gospel other than the one we preached to you, let him be eternally condemned!"* (Galatians 1:8 NIV). The Bible establishes the rules and norms for our faith because it was written for our gain. There is no other authority on the face of the earth. There is no other book like the Bible. The Bible is the way that leads us to obey the words of the Master, delivering us from falling into disobedience, deceitfulness and lies, and even from following doctrines of perversion and error which today, unfortunately, roam in many so called "Christian churches", even amongst many "prosperous" ministries. Some have distorted God's Word for their own personal gain. *"And we also thank God continually because, when you received the word of God, which you heard from us, you accepted it not as the word of men, but as it actually is, the word of God, with is at work in you who believe*" (1 Thessalonians 2:13 NIV). The Bible is God's Word!

4 — The Bible must be read entirely and never be altered

God's eternal purpose is that we cite the Bible just as it reads. What God wanted to reveal to us through the Bible, is written in its pages. Nowadays, there are "ministries" that receive daily "new revelations from God." And among these "ministries", there is an impressive competition as to "who receives the greatest revelations." In doing this, they completely forsake the Bible. Their hearts feed on their own "revelations." I don't find a reason why these so called "revelations" shouldn't be included in the next edition of the New Testament. If they are so important, and if they come from God, then, all of God's people need to hear them. Now, if these revelations are not sacred, as the Word of God is; they are deceptions and lies that are birthed out of ministerial self-promotion. What God wanted to reveal of Himself to mankind is what we call the Canon, which is the group of sixty-six books in the Bible, inspired and revealed by God. Everything else is a fantasy, guile and lies of these false "revelatory ministers." *"The secret things belong to the Lord our God, but the things revealed belong to us and to our children forever, that we may follow all the words of this law*" (Deuteronomy 29:29 NIV). What law? Which things revealed? It's talking about God's Word, the Bible, which is God's revelation to us; everything else is human invention. We must not add anything to the Bible, nor take away from it. The Bible is what it is! Hallelujah!

"Hear now, O Israel, the decrees and laws I am about to teach you. Follow them so that you may live...Do not add to what I com-

mand you and do not subtract from it, but keep the commands of the Lord your God that I give you" (Deuteronomy 4:1-2 NIV). God commanded to not alter and take away from the Scriptures. And what God ordained should be obeyed. Chapter 12 of the same Book declares: *"See that you do all I command you; do not add to it or take away from it"* (Deuteronomy 12:32 NIV). We must be very careful not to add or take away words or verses from the Bible.

One time, a young Christian man was traveling by train. Sitting next to him was a young man reading the Bible. The first one asked him if what he was reading was the Word of God, to which the second politely replied, yes. Then the young man noticed that the Bible was very thin and not thick like the other ones he had seen before. So he asked: Why is your Bible so small and not like the other Bibles, or like mine? So, the young man with the thin Bible replied: "Our Church has an intellectual pastor; each time he preaches and doesn't agree with a Scripture in the Bible, he instructs us to tear out the verses or the pages, and what you are seeing is what's left of the original Book." This is ridiculous! But unfortunately true! Many churches and "ministers" no longer desire to do, obey and preach God's Word as it is. The apostle Paul said to us in his writing of wisdom to the young Timothy: *"Preach the Word; be prepared in season and out of season; correct, rebuke and encourage—with great patience and careful instruction...They will turn their ears away from the truth and turn aside to myths"* (2 Timothy 4:2,4 NIV). Unfortunately, today, in the United States, there are churches that have completely abandoned the true preaching of God's Word in their services. They no longer speak against immorality; quite to the contrary, they support those who live in perversion, to the point of accepting homosexual marriages, while God established that marriage should only be performed between a man and a woman. (Genesis 2:24-25; Romans 1:24,26,29) These churches are very rich and powerful, financially speaking, but have been deceived by the devil. The Word for them is the same one spoken to the church of Laodicea: *"You say, 'I am rich; I have acquired wealth and do not need a thing. But you do not realize that you are wretched, pitiful, poor, blind and naked"* (Revelation 3:17 NIV). God deliver us from preaching anything else than His Word—the Bible! We must preach it just as it is, and not as we think or personally interpret it.

"Do not add to his words, or he will rebuke you and prove you a liar" (Proverbs 30:6 NIV). According to this Scripture, we conclude that all those who don't preach the Word with truth, specially those famous speakers that receive such "revelations", are liars and deceivers. We need to be honest and truthful when we minister the words out of the Holy Book, with all diligence, reverence and integrity from our part.

There was a church that had a terrible preacher. During his sermons he would say things that were not in the Bible, and he always added or took away something from the Scriptures. One day, while he was giving his sermon, he said: "Chapter 10 of Malachi, says thus and such ..." A sister in the congregation called out, "Mr. Preacher, the Book of Malachi only has four chapters!" To what the preacher replied: "I know, but the Lord revealed to me these verses..." The truth is God didn't reveal a thing to this man; he just didn't know the Scriptures. Be careful in doing things like this; it's very dangerous to change the Scripture to our advantage. The Book of Revelation declares: *"I warn everyone who hears the words of the prophecy of this book: If anyone adds anything to them, God will add to him the plagues described in this book. And if anyone takes words away from this book of prophecy, God will take away from him his share in the tree of life and in the holy city, which are described in this book"* (Revelation 22:18-19 NIV). Adding or taking away words from the Scripture is a matter of life or death.

One time, a little girl while having lunch with her mother asked:

— Mom, who does the Bible belong to?

Kindly, the mother replied:

— The Bible belongs to God, sweetie.

Then she replied:

— Then why don't we just give it back to Him; nobody in this house uses it.

It's sad to hear that many people hardly ever read the Scripture. It's my prayer that we would love the Scriptures as in the beginning, because it's the power that fuels our spiritual life and the means by which we learn from God.

The Bible says that the Scribes, Sadducees and Pharisees studied the Scriptures; they were learned, but they never came to the knowledge of the true revealed Word of God. Matthew, the evangelist, declared: *"One of them, an expert in the law, tested him…"* (Matthew 22:35 NIV). They were wise and knowledgeable in the written Word, they studied meticulously, with dedication and reverence, but they were never able to understand, discern and accept that Christ was the fulfillment of those same Scriptures that they had studied so long.

They were blind, and unable to recognize that Christ brought life into the writings with His coming. It's dangerous to study the Scriptures without the proper discernment of the Holy Spirit. For this reason, so many people, after studying them, fell into their own interpretations and created new cults, doctrines and false religions, for they desired to apply their own point of view to Scripture, which is divine and completely accurate.. This is why the Apostle Paul said: *"He has made us competent as ministers of a new covenant — not of the letter but of the Spirit; for the letter kills, but the Spirit gives life"* (2 Corinthians 3:6 NIV). The religious intellectualism of certain "ministers" has driven them into pride, arrogance, and an intolerable egotism in their words and actions behind the pulpit. These ministers, having the desire to become greater than their ministry colleagues, and imposing their intellectualism against the principles of humility, have become unbearable fools, dry, empty, and dead in their spiritual lives. It's not that I'm against secular or theological preparation. No, quite to the contrary. However, it doesn't matter how great of a student of the Word we become, nevertheless, we must never ignore the place of the Holy Spirit, because it is He who can give us accurate discernment and the correct application that will avail our sermons with power, wisdom and the true authority of God's Word. We must preach the Word with humility, acknowledging that only God, through His grace, can make us ministers of the new covenant. For this reason, Paul also affirmed: *"But we have this treasure in jars of clay to show that this all-surpassing power is from God and not from us"* (2 Corinthians 4:7 NIV). The glory belongs to God! And as I've always said in pastoral or missionary conferences: First, God calls; Second, God equips; Third, God sends; Fourth, God provides; And Fifth, God follows with signs. Everything belongs to God! In and out of ourselves, we have nothing. We must not take God's place. If we do, we are diminishing the Scriptures for Paul said that the power is of God and not of ourselves. D.L. Moody's ministry secret resided in the following verse, to which he often attributed the success to his ministry: "*...that power belongeth unto God*" (Psalm 62:11 KJV). It's God's Power!

I would like to close this chapter with a brief story. A long time ago, a man of God traveled to the Soviet Union to deliver a Bible shipment. This happened during communist rule. In his Moscow hotel room he noticed that he had lost the piece of paper where the address of his contact was written. That man had such a relationship with God that taking a pencil and a piece of paper in his hand, he said to the Lord:

—O.K. Lord, I lost the address, but I would like for you to tell me where I can find this pastor; you tell me, and I'll write it down.

God answered:

—It doesn't work that way! Who lost the address? Was it you, or I?

The man of God replied:

—I lost it!

And God said to him:

—Then you find it! And God also said: Pray and fast for three days, and I will tell you where he is.

After the three days, the man of God said:

—I'm ready Lord! Tell me, and I'll write.

The Lord said:

—It doesn't work that way! Get up and go sit down on a bench at the Red Square, and there I will tell you where to find the pastor.

The man began questioning God:

—Why can't you just tell me here in my room? Does it have to be out in the cold and snow?

The Lord replied:

—Because that is the place where I want to tell you, and not here.

Then, the man of God got up and went to the Red Square. And as soon as he sat down, a guard approached him and began interrogating him:

—What are you doing here alone? Show me your passport!

The man of God was praying in the spirit to the Lord and saying:

—Look at the mess I'm in now and all because you didn't want to spell the address out to me in the room. Of all places, I had to come here!

The policeman asked:

—What are you doing in the Soviet Union?

The man of God said that he had come to visit and do some tourism, etc... At that time, God said to him:

—Don't be a liar! Tell the guard what you came to do.

The man of God answered:

—But Lord, how am I going to say a thing like that?

God said:

—Tell him right now!

So he got up from the bench and said:

—Very well! I am a minister of the gospel. I came to bring a Bible shipment; I lost the address of the pastor who was my contact. Now, you can take me to prison.

The guard, smiling and putting his hand on the man of God's shoulder said:

—I already saw your name on the passport. Where was the man of God? We have been waiting for three days. The pastor you are looking for is my father. You see me in this military uniform because we all are drafted into the army, but I'm a believer in Jesus, and my father is the pastor who's been waiting for you for three days. Where were you?

God is faithful! He will never allow any of His Words

to go unfulfilled. He said that He would keep us in all of our ways. This man was smuggling Bibles, taking God's blessed Word behind the Iron Curtain, and God's protection was with him all the time. *"The Lord said to me, 'you have seen correctly for I am watching to see that my word is fulfilled.* (Jeremiah 1:12 NIV).

God wrote the Bible for a very specific purpose in our lives. He made sure to leave us the Book that would lead us to know him, and would guide us into eternal life. God is so marvelous, compassionate, merciful, faithful, and great in power and glory. It's necessary to point out that many people have not given the greatest priority to God's Word. Let's make a quality decision to read and study it, giving it a place of prominence in our hearts.

Chapter Five

A Mandate to God's People

"It is to be with him, and he is to read it all the days of his life so that he may learn to revere the Lord his God and follow carefully all the words of this law and these decrees" (Deuteronomy 17:19 NIV).

When my children were very small, my wife and I taught them to respect pastors, evangelists, ministers, and all of God's servants. We endeavored to guide them in these teachings so that Kathryn would some day become a woman of God, and Junior, a prophet and preacher of God's Word. We taught them that they must not point their fingers at a minister, accuse him of shortcomings, or criticize him, etc... We explained this to them at their own age level so they could understand.

One day, Kathy and Junior were playing in their room, and it was very late and they had to sleep. They were jumping, hollering and playing with their dolls. So I stood at the door of their room and said: "It's bed time. Each one goes to their room." Then I returned to the living room to continue talking with Damaris. After a few minutes, I realized that they were still playing. We could hear the laughter and sing-a-longs with their dolls. So, I returned to the room and said: "OK, who am I going to start disciplining today? Which one of you will be first?" I looked at Junior and said: "You are the youngest one, and the rascal; I'm going to start with you..." Kathryn, seeing that her brother was in trouble, put herself in a covering position over his body, looked at me, and said: "You can't discipline Junior! You shouldn't spank him either!" So, I asked her why not. To what she replied: "Because Junior is a prophet and a servant of God, and God's servants and prophets shouldn't be disciplined, they are not to be whipped and no harm should come to them…" Children are great! What a way of applying what we instructed them to their own benefit.

In this chapter we will deal with the importance of receiving instruction, studying, preaching and being faithful to the Scriptures.

1 — The study of God's Word is a mandate to us.

God has charged us to study His Word. This is a mandate, not a suggestion. The study of God's Word is a divine directive that must not be substituted with anything else. In any profession or career, study is required. If you desire to understand how computers work, you must study computer sciences. If you desired to become an airplane pilot, you would need to go to flight school. If you aspire to become a medical doctor, you must study medicine. The same if you want to become a dentist, you must study dentistry, and so forth. The ministry is the same scenario; if you desire to become a minister of God, you must study the Scripture; if you don't, you'll fail. It's impossible to calculate the damage that has been done by workers who are improperly prepared. Some have even gone out without basic instruction to labor in the Lord's missionary field, without even knowing the Lord of the field. There are men and women who labor in the ministry without knowing the God of their ministry. Workers that preach the Word without understanding the Word they preach. Some have caused great conflict, confusion and ruin in the Christian field.

God said to the nation of Israel that one of the king's responsibilities is to read the Word every day. This way he would fear God in all of his ways. God says to every believer and to those of us ministers of His Word, that every day we must read the Bible. In the Book of Deuteronomy we read that in reading His Word, we would be able to live it out. It also says reading His Word would deliver us from pride: *"...and not to consider himself better than his brothers..."* (Deuteronomy 17:20 NIV). This is the antidote against self-importance, pride, arrogance and haughtiness. The Word of God will make us humble, and dependent upon Him every day. Studying the Scriptures, we come to the conclusion that we are weak and powerless without God and His help. We perceive the fragility of life before the greatness and power of God's presence. The psalmist declares: *"All our days pass away...the length of our days...yet the span is but trouble and sorrow, for they quickly pass, and we fly away. Teach us to number our days aright, that we may gain a heart of wisdom"* (Psalm 90: 9-10, 12 NIV). O, we are fragile!

One time, a pastor preached about verse twelve in this psalm. During the whole sermon, he pointed out that we are ashes and dust. It was a Sunday morning and the church was full. In closing his sermon, he asked the congregation: "What are we?" And in one voice all replied: "We are ashes and dust, ashes and dust..." When the pastor finished, he called a deacon to pray and close the service. In his prayer, the deacon said: "Lord, remember that I'm dust, my wife is dust and so are my children. Finally, have mercy upon your dusty Church, because we are all ashes and dust..." That's what we are: dust!

After our physical death we will be reduced to dust. What are we then? Nothing! When we consider our frailty, we should conclude that the study of the Scriptures is a mandate for us. In reading the Bible, the Lord instructs us to walk in wisdom and dependency upon Him. We need to study and probe the Scriptures. Let's read what the prophet Isaiah teaches us: *"Look in the scroll of the Lord and read"* (Isaiah 34:16 NIV). We need to seek, study, investigate and make God's Word the source for our answers, in order to understand his pursuits. Jesus himself, in the Gospel of John, spoke of the importance of studying the Scriptures: *"...Diligently study the Scriptures because you think that by them you possess eternal life. These are the Scriptures that testify about me..."* (John 5:39 NIV).

When king Zedekiah needed to hear a Word from the Lord during an imminent crisis his nation, Israel, was facing, the Bible declares: "Then king Zedekiah...asked him secretly, in his home: Is there a Word from the Lord?" Yes, there is. God always desires to speak to our heart; there's always a Word from the Lord for us. But to be able to hear Him, we must return to the Scriptures, and study, seek, and make them a priority in our lives. We must seek, study, and investigate them. We need to have the mindset the Bereans had: *"Now the Bereans were of more noble character than the Thessalonians, for they received the message with great eagerness and examined the Scriptures every day to see if what Paul said was true"* (Acts 17:11 NIV). Nobility doesn't consist in being born into a royal family, or that of a rich or powerful earthly king. No! Jesus was born in a manger. He could have been born in a palace because, in reality, He is King; however, he was born in a poor and humble place. His nobility resided in the fact that He was the revelation of God's Word made flesh. The Bible says that the

Berean people were more noble...because the examined the Scriptures every day to see if what Paul and Silas said was true or not. In the light of this scripture, we can say that nobleness in the eyes of God is to have esteem and appreciation for the Bible. To love it as we love ourselves. When we examine the Scriptures, we learn what happened to the kings of Israel and Judah when they forsake the Word. Although they were born into nobility and displayed their privilege of being kings, they were all destroyed for turning their backs on God and for not ruling in accordance with His Word. The Bible declares that Joash began to reign in Jerusalem when he seven years old. At the beginning of his reign, he did what was right in the eyes of the Lord, but he later abandoned the God of Israel. He started right but ended wrong. Let's read what the Book of Chronicles declares: *"They abandoned the temple of the Lord, the God of their fathers...although the Lord sent prophets to the people to bring them back to him...they wouldn't listen. Then the Spirit of the Lord came upon Zechariah...He stood before the people and said: 'Why do you disobey the Lord's commands?' But they plotted against him, and by order of the king they stoned him to death in the courtyard of the Lord's temple"* (2 Chronicles 24:18-21 NIV). Joash turned his back on the Lord to the point of killing a prophet of God. Why? Because he gave up loving, respecting and obeying the Word of God as he had done in the beginning of his reign. Many ministers have started out right but ended wrong. So many ministers have grown, and when they became great, they abandoned the Lord and His Word. How many churches started out small, and grew to a thousand members. But, unfortunately, as time went by, they slowly abandoned the principles of God's Word, and the fear of God, only to allow liberalism and the world's philosophy into the lives of their members, corrupting the Church, its doctrine and holiness; without which, no one will see the Lord.

How many immigrants have come to the United States from Latin-America and the rest of the world, surrendering their lives to the Lord and asking Him to prosper them because they came to this country with nothing. And when God poured out His blessings upon them, prospering them in their businesses and great opportunities, they abandoned God forgetting His goodness and mercy, and forsaking His Word. Today, these people are no longer in Church but backslidden without God and faith, living only for the things of this world and their self-fulfillment.

How many believers started out living right and running their Christian race, but as time went by they fell into sin, and instead of coming back to the Word, they completely forsook it. If you see them today, their lives are in ruin and they are away from God's house, with no joy, happiness, peace, and what is worst, without the assurance of eternal life, running the risk of dying at any moment and facing eternity without Christ.

Dear reader, if you find yourself afar draw near to Christ right now. He will forgive you. Leave your problems, deeds, and hurts at the foot of the cross. He is the God of second chances. Jesus said: *"Come to me, all you who are weary and burdened, and I will give you rest"* (Matthew 11:28 NIV). Come back to Him today! And if you are a believer, but have abandoned some of the principles of God's Word, come back to them right now. Come back to the joy of serving Christ, sharing His Word with others, for your pastor will be waiting to help you. To know Christ is to rejoice and be blessed. To know God's Word is marvelous. To live in harmony and unity with other ministers is beautiful; to share our experiences with other pastors, and being friends one with another is a great pleasure: *"How good and pleasant it is when brothers live together in unity! For there the Lord bestows his blessing, even life forevermore"* (Psalm 133:1,3 NIV). I have a few friends who are pastors and ministers with whom I spend hours talking and learning from, and sometimes, we remember funny memories that make us laugh and hug each other.

One time, three evangelical ministers who were friends with each other, got together at one of their homes to have lunch. And although they were part of different denominations, they always upheld respect, harmony and friendship among themselves. Despite their theological differences they had prayed together and shared the things of God for many years. They frequently they invited each other to preach for special occasions. However, on this particular occasion, the wife of one of them prepared succulent barbecued pork. After one of the pastors finished praying for the blessing over the meal, another colleague had an idea that only those who agreed with his game would be able to eat the barbecued pork, and whoever played the best would get the best part of the pork. So another one said: "Let's see who knows more of the Word!" The first pastor, who was a Presbyterian started out by saying: "The Bible declares that Peter had a sword, so he swung it and injured the high priest's servant, cutting off his right ear. His name was Malchus". So the pastor took a knife, cut the pork's ears, and placed them on his plate. Very good! Said the other pastors. The second pastor, who was a Baptist, said: "Well, the Bible also says that king Herod the Tetrarch, ordered that John the Baptist's head be cut off, and brought to him on a plate." And the third pastor, who was an Assembly of God minister, concluded and said: "And to finish off the sequence of events of that spoken by my Baptist colleague, the Bible says: "John's disciples came and took his body and buried it." Everybody laughed, and the pastor reaching over said: "If you will all excuse me, I will take the barbecued pork's body home and bury it in my stomach."

It's so good to have friendships. There is a time for everything. Ministers also need to laugh and have fun, and take a trip with their family, because ministry demands a lot of time. Our work has many facets, and we can become worn out mentally, physically, and emotionally.

2 — The preaching of God's Word is a mandate to us.

The Word of God is a seed that we must sow. Even though we sow in weariness, and weeping with a wounded heart, as the psalmist said: *"He who goes out weeping, carrying seed to sow, will return with songs of joy, carrying sheaves with him"* (Psalm 125:6 NIV). How many times I feel tired, after preaching a crusade of one or two weeks, on the other side of the world! Sometimes financially blessed, sometimes not, with the weariness of not sleeping due to the time zones. The day of my return I check out of the hotel totally exhausted from not sleeping well, with headaches, weakness, and with hunger simply because I've not had time to eat. Then I take a flight that takes two to three hours to make a connection. Many times flights are cancelled and I get delayed a day or so, only to arrive home in total physical exhaustion, but full of joy. Happy for the souls that got saved, for the healing miracles that took place, and for the power of the Spirit that was poured out, knowing that I will see those who I love: my dear wife

Damaris and my children Kathryn and Junior, the most precious treasures I have on this earth. One of my favorite psalms is 128:

> *Blessed are all who fear the Lord, who walk in his ways. Your will eat the fruit of your labor; blessings and prosperity will be yours. Your wife will be like a fruitful vine within your house; your sons will be like olive shoots around your table. Thus is the man blessed who fears the Lord.*

In this same Psalm God says to us: *"and may you live to see your children's children"* (v.6) I desire to live many years. I want to see my children get married, if the Lord tarries to come back for His Church, I want to dedicate my grandchildren to the Lord, as my parents did with me. I always want to serve God with my family. Damaris is a preacher of the Word as well, and Kathryn sings and leads worship in children's church; Junior has been preaching little sermons since he was five, and surely he will become a great preacher of the Gospel. What else could I ask for? I don't need anything else. I'm happy! I'm blessed because I fear the Lord. I only want to preach God's Word to the whole world, at any place that He leads me to, as I've already done in every continent.

My desire is to win a lost world to Christ. As Hudson Taylor, a great missionary to China who ministered fifty years in that nation once said: "If I had one thousand lives, I would give them for China". This is my goal. I don't want anything else. I would say, as David Brainerd of the United States said: "I rejoice in my personal abnegation, having what to eat, or not; having clothes to dress, or not; I don't care. I want to win the souls of the Indians for Christ." I would also say as John Knox said, the great

Scottish reformer: "Give me Scotland or I'll die…" And I will speak as Zinzendorf: "I have great passions, Christ and souls, give me souls, souls, and more souls…" And I will finish repeating the words of Dr. David Livingstone, the great missionary to the African continent, who declared: "God had an only Son, Jesus Christ, and that Son was a missionary. As long as I live, I will be a missionary…" Our calling is: To preach God's Word.

A rainy Saturday afternoon, Edward Kimball heard the voice of the Holy Spirit and ran to the small shop where D.L. Moody was working as a cobbler. Kimball won D.L. Moody for Christ, and D.L Moody became a Sunday school teacher. Later, this simple cobbler became a famous preacher to multitudes, in England as well as in the United States. Moody became a great soul winner. This is our goal: we are preachers of God's Word. The Bible contains the message we must proclaim. We don't need to seek for another book as an auxiliary help to preach our messages; God's Word is enough. It is sufficient and we don't need to preach any other subject, but the Gospel of Christ. In the book "The biblical theology of missions", Dr. Hugh Thompson says:

We are not sent to preach sociology but salvation. We aren't sent to preach economy but evangelism. We haven't been called to preach reform but redemption. We haven't been commissioned to preach culture but conversion. We are not here to preach progress but forgiveness. We have not received the commission to preach a new social order but a new birth. We don't preach revolution but regeneration. We should never preach about our organization, but rather about the new creation in Christ. We don't preach about a democracy but about the gospel; and finally, we haven't been redeemed to preach about a new civilization but the remission of our sins through the Lord Jesus Christ.

Let's read what the apostle Paul says in his second letter to the Corinthians: *"For we do not preach ourselves, but Jesus Christ the Lord"* (2 Corinthians 4:5 NIV). We need to preach Christ, His power, authority, love, forgiveness and victory on the cross. When we consider the world's situation, we perceive the great responsibility that we have to reach the world for Christ, which takes us to the conclusion that preaching God's Word is a mandate for us. In 1992, I was invited to teach about the mission field by the Latin American Department of William Carey University at the World Missions Center in Pasadena, California, I considered it a great honor to be able to influence the minds of young hearts and minds that are willing to become future preachers of God's Word in foreign lands and at home. Many of my students—now excellent preachers—reside in foreign lands and have faithfully obeyed Christ's call to the mission field.

Alexander Mackay, writing to the Society of Missionary Churches, wrote: "My heart burns for Africa's freedom" Reinhard Bonnke, an evangelist that God has raised extraordinarily, once said: "Africa is not going to be saved; Africa is being saved." He travels all over the African continent, and during his crusades there have been well over a million people, at one time, in one place. God is pouring out his power into every continent through a worldwide revival. Bonnke preaches the simple gospel with the power of God's Word and the results are enormous. That's what the Bible contains: the simple message of the Gospel. Just as Billy Graham, these evangelists are very successful because they preach the simple message of the Gospel in the power of God's Word. By media such as audiotapes and videos, we have ministered in one hundred twelve countries, and many people have been saved and radically transformed as a result of preaching the simple message of the Gospel. We receive daily e-mails from people telling us how their lives have been changed by hearing our messages; how their children and families have come to know Christ; and how entire churches have been transformed and revived, as well as how pastors and ministers have been edified after showing our messages on a big screen in their churches, or in the privacy of their homes. This is the extraordinary effect of God's Word when it's preached with simplicity and with the anointing of the Holy Spirit.

Melvin Cox, a missionary to Liberia who died just four months after he arrived, said before his death: "May thousands fall before one of us quits and Africa is lost." We can't quit our endeavor to evangelize the world. We need to unite our denominational efforts for the same purpose: Lead the lost to Christ, in any way, or possible form, with any evangelistic strategy that God grants us, in whatever project it may be, using the Bible as the central message in every single endeavor.

When Henry Martin arrived in India, he said: "Let me be ablaze, give my all, consume myself for God, for God and India." O that we may say the same! That our love be greater for the lost than for ourselves. That we would be able to lay aside all selfishness and personal interests and renounce to "I" and that we would be able to say like Martin: "O God I want to be consumed for you…" And to also say in our own words: "Give us, Lord, our beloved nation. Save Europe. Pour out your power upon this continent that is cold and hostile to your word. Save Africa and break it's curses. Save Asia and destroy the false gods that exist in that continent. Save the Americas, from Alaska to Chile, and raise up an army of missionaries in Latin America. O God, save Australia and New Zealand, use those whose hearts are willing to go there. Lord, use us to save a lost and dying world." I pray that we would never forget God's cry in the book of Isaiah:

Then I heard the voice of the Lord saying, *"Whom shall I send? And who will go for us? And I said, "Here am I, Send me!"* (Isaiah 6:8-9 NIV).

We don't need to wait for a supernatural calling. He has already called us through His Word when He said go! We only need to be obedient. The Bible commissions, orders us, and sends us to preach the Gospel. This is not an option, but a command. As a missionary in Madrid, Spain, between 1983-1984, with YWAM, I learned of Keith Green's songs, a Christian singer who went on to be with the Lord in a tragic airplane accident. One of the songs that blessed my life, and that I hold among my favorite ones, is the song "Jesus commands me to go!" In it's lyrics it says:

Jesus commands us to go, but we go the other way. So He carries the burden alone, while His children are busy at play, feeling so called to stay. Oh, how God grieves and believes that the world can't be saved, unless the ones He's appointed obey, His command and His stand for the world, that He loved more than life. Oh He died, and he cries out tonight. Jesus commands us to go, it should be the exception if we stay. It's no wonder we're moving so slow when His church refuses to obey, feeling so called to stay. Oh how God comes, as He starts the great judgment of fire, so He can gain, His Greatest desire. Cause He knows that the souls of the lost, they can only be reached, through us, we're His hands and His feet. Jesus commands us to go...

The Apostle Paul said: *"Woe to me if I do not preach the Gospel!"* (1 Corinthians 9:16 NIV) We should take up our Bible in a spirit of praise and adoration and use it as a sword. *"May the praise of God be in their mouths and a double-edged sword in their hands"* (Psalm 149:6 NIV). The Bible contains seed that we must sow. *"The farmer sows the word. Some people are like seed along the path, where the word is sown"* (Mark 4:14-15 NIV). The Scriptures must be the foundation of every message that we preach; anything else is not approved for the task of preaching. And God will bless us when we faithfully do it: *"Now he who supplies seed to the sower and bread for food will also supply and increase your store of seed and will enlarge the harvest of your righteousness"* (2 Corinthians 9:10 NIV). He called us to preach His Word.

3 — Trusting in His Word is a mandate to us.

The Word of God is totally true and reliable. The faithfulness of Scripture surpasses our understanding. Whatever God said he would do, He will. Let's read what the first book of Kings says: *"Praise be to the Lord, who has given rest to his people Israel just as he promised. Not one word has failed of all the good promises he gave through his servant Moses"* (1 Kings 8:56 NIV). When has God failed? Did He ever fail to fulfill His promises? When He promised something, did He not come through? God is faithful, and His Word is true. He has never failed and never will! To err is human, man does fail, but God is divine. *"This is a trustworthy saying that deserves full acceptance"* (1 Timothy 4:9 NIV). Eschatology is the study of prophecies and their relationship with the end times. When we study eschatology, we can perceive the truth of God's Word and how reliable it is. Many events have come to pass before our own eyes; the events associated with the nation of Israel and the Second Coming of Christ. Everything is coming to pass exactly as Jesus said. Trusting in His Word is a mandate to us.

> *"Your statutes stand firm; holiness adorns your house for endless days, O Lord"*

> Psalm 93:5 NIV

When a builder begins to build a house, a commercial building or a bridge, the first thing that is laid down is the foundation, by a process of bonding iron and concrete into a solid mass. The construction is then founded on pillars that are buried deep enough to support the weight of the walls. Its base is solid and firmly established so that the construction will stand. The Bible is our base and foundation. It's as firm as a spiritual pillar buried deep solidly in our hearts to withstand any problem or adversity that we may face. He will make us stand forever no matter what we face today or tomorrow. *"The works of his hands are faithful and just; all his precepts are trustworthy..."* (Psalm 111:7 NIV) The Bible states that all of its laws, commandments and promises are faithful. The Words of the Lord are trustworthy of faith; they're reliable, true, accurate, and they never fail. In the book of the prophet Ezekiel we find this truth confirmed again:

> *"But I the Lord will speak what I will, and it shall be fulfilled without delay. For in your days, you rebel-*

lious house, I will fulfill whatever I say, declares the Sovereign Lord"

Ezekiel 12:25 NIV

If God promised something, He will bring it to pass. However, if you don't do your part of obeying the Word, don't expect His promises to come to pass in your life. Some people say to me: "Brother Yrión, God spoke to me many years ago and said that He would use me, but nothing of that has occurred to this day." Then I ask: "Did you fulfill what was required of you for Him to fulfill His promises." And I hear: "O, uhmm… OK." This is their response. How real are the words of the prophet Isaiah! "You rebellious house". Our rebellions have consequences. Let's read what the prophet Daniel says:

> *You have fulfilled words spoken against us…Just as it is written in the Law of Moses, all this disaster has come upon us, yet we have not sought the favor of the Lord our God by turning from our sins…For the Lord our God is righteous in everything he does; yet we have not obeyed him."*

Daniel 9:12-14 NIV

Whatever God has promised, he will fulfill it for better or worse. If we obey and trust in His Word, He will fulfill what He said for best. But if we disobey His Word, He will fulfill what he said to bring on judgment and destruction. The choice is yours! If we despise His Word, He will despise us. *"Because he has despised the Lord's word and broken his commands, that person must surely be cut off; his guilt remains on him"* (Numbers 15:31 NIV).

Some Pentecostal organizations, instead of trusting and preaching the Word of God "as it is", invalidate the real content and effectiveness of God's Word by rules of man and precepts of the founders that established them. Many of these precepts are against the move of the Spirit, and they take us to recall Jesus' warning: *"...These people honor me with their lips, but their hearts are far from me. They worship me in vain; their teachings are but rules taught by men. You have let go of the commands of God and are holding on to the traditions of men... You have a fine way of setting aside the commands of God in order to observe your own traditions! Thus you nullify the word of God by your tradition that you have handed down. And you do many things like that"* (Mark 7:6-9,13 NIV).

The Pentecostal movement has suffered innumerable absurd Pharisaic prohibitions that posses no effectiveness against the desires of the flesh. Our emphasis must always be the Word of God, putting all of our trust in it to overcome in every spiritual battle that we have with the kingdom of darkness. The Apostle Paul teaches us about the ridiculousness of the legalistic precepts of men in writing to the Colossians:

"...Why, as though you still belonged to it, do you submit to its rules: 'Do not handle! Do not taste! Do not touch!' (In conformity to commandments and doctrines of men), These are all destined to perish with use, because they are based on human commands and teachings. Such regulations indeed have an appearance of wisdom, with their self-imposed worship, their false humility and their harsh treatment of the body, but they lack any value in restraining sensual indulgence"

Colossians 2:20-23 NIV

For this reason, many churches of our time have weakened the lives of their members; because, the pastors, instead of preaching God's Word, have preached insults and offenses to those who do not agree with "their ideas" or doctrinal "messages". Instead of winning souls for Christ, they cast them into hell nullifying God's love and mercy, leading their hearers into a spiritual death. Well said the Apostle Paul in his letter to the Romans: *"It is not as though God's word had failed"* (Romans 9:6 NIV). The Word of God never fails; it's the preacher who fails when he teaches "personal absurd doctrines", repelling people by the harshness of his words.

In his second letter to the Corinthians, the Apostle Paul declares, *"the weapons we fight with are not the weapons of the world. On the contrary, they have divine power to demolish strongholds"* (2 Corinthians 10:4 NIV). We cannot use the weapons of the "flesh" to destroy and overcome the flesh, but only those of the Spirit. We need to trust in the Word, and not in something without a biblical base. When we preach or hear the Word as it is, we will have extraordinary results and we will fear the Lord: *"Hear the word of the Lord, you who tremble at his word"* (Isaiah 66:5 NIV). Do you tremble at His Word? There are those who think they are smarter rejecting the words of God that are in the Scriptures. What they don't understand is that they're heaping condemnation to themselves. *"The wise will be put to shame; they will be dismayed and trapped. Since they have rejected the word of the Lord, what kind of wisdom do they have?"* (Jeremiah 8:9 NIV). True wisdom is founded in trusting, loving, and fearing the Lord and His Word. Just because we trust in God's Word, some heathens and people of the world scorn us as the arrogant people in the days of the prophet Jeremiah: *"Where is the word of the Lord? Let it now be fulfilled!"* (Jeremiah 17:15 NIV). But the day will come when they will run to find a church, because their problems, diseases, afflictions and needs will be so great that only God will be able to help them.

I pray that God helps us to understand that the secret to victory is in trusting His Word, and not in ourselves. During 1985 when traveling in the communist countries of Eastern Europe, I was on a train because it was safer to cross borders by that means, and cheaper too. When the train arrived into Sofia Station, capital of Bulgaria, a young man traveling from Rumania sat by my side. He took a book out of his handbag and began reading. I turned to see the title, which was written in red "The Socialist World". After a while of having my Bible in hand, I asked him: "What are you reading?" To what the young man replied: "I'm reading about 'our' socialist world". We introduced each other and began a conversation. He was from Yugoslavia. When he learned I was from Brazil, he quickly asked about the Brazilian national team and soccer, because in his country, at that time, they were discussing the elimination process for the World Cup, which was carried out the following year in Mexico. After an extensive chat about many subjects, I perceived there was an open door, just because I was Brazilian and, by his words, Brazil was "Soccerland". I felt it was a good time to introduce him to the Gospel, and without hesitation, I asked him:

—This book that you hold in your hands, did it give you peace?

Then, he opened his heart and said:

—I'm a professor of Socialism, I teach Lenin and Marx at the University of Belgrade, and I have a vacuum in my heart, which nothing to this date has been able to fill it; not even socialism.

Due to his sincere and honest response I said:

—I'm a preacher of the Gospel and I'm going to introduce you to the only person who can fill the emptiness of your heart with love and peace. His name is Jesus Christ.

Then he exclaimed:

—That's why I saw you with your Bible in your hand... You are not allowed to speak of Christ on this train; it's full of soldiers, and you're in a Communist country (Bulgaria).

I replied:

—No problem, I'm not afraid of them, and nothing is going to happen. Right now, you are more important than they are.

After thirty or forty-five minutes, admitting that communism was not the answer nor the truth, that young man, with tears in his eyes hearing the simple Gospel of Christ for the first time in his life, totally opened his heart to trust in God's Word, and gave his life to Christ. Immediately after he repeated the sinner's prayer with my arm on his shoulder, right there, on the train's seat, he was born again on a July afternoon of 1985.

The Lord destroyed the stronghold of socialism in the mind of that young man. As Paul said:

"We demolish arguments and every pretension that sets itself up against the knowledge of God, and we take captive every thought (ideas, philosophies, doctrines and systems) to make it obedient to Christ."

2 Corinthians 10:5 NIV

These are the results we get when we trust in the Word. If you trust the Word, it will transform your life, it will fill the vacuum inside of you, it will shatter your doubts and unbelief, you will be delivered from fear, and it will help you to face your adversities. It will lead you to all truth, setting you free from false doctrines, cults and religions of deception: of the worldly systems and pseudo-philosophies. It will set you apart from the ideas that are contrary to the Scriptures, taking you to a place of peace and tranquility for your soul, assuring you eternal life with Jesus Christ the Lord. This is the power of God's Word!

4 — The teaching of God's Word is a mandate to us

The Lord Jesus charges us to correctly receive the teachings of His word. Let's read what the Apostle Paul urges to his son in the faith, Timothy:

> *"You, however, know all about my teaching...but as for you, continue in what you have learned..."*

2 Timothy 3:10a, 14 NIV

Every one of us has learned the Word through someone: *"For I received from the Lord what I also passed on to you"* (1 Corinthians 11:23 NIV). From the moment that we learn God's Word through someone, like the Corinthians learned from Paul, then we can teach to the members of our family, and others as well. First learn the principles in Scripture, then we teach and share with others. As parents, we must rightly teach our children. The Word teaches:

> *"Remember the day you stood before the Lord your God at Horeb, when he said to me, "Assemble the people before me to hear my words so that they may learn to revere me as long as they live in the land and may teach them to their children."*

Deuteronomy 4:10 NIV

If we have faith and fear God in our hearts, we will put that into our children; and if we know the Word, we will also impart that to our children. In the book of Deuteronomy we read about the teaching of the Scripture: *"Teach them to your children, taking about them"* (Deuteronomy 11:19 NIV). I'm investing in Kathryn and Junior's life. And I'm sure that one day they will serve the Lord in a great way. They will inherit my experiences and the wisdom I have acquired throughout these years. They will inherit Damaris' experiences and the wisdom that she has received from her parents and of the testimonies acquired in Cuba, during her childhood, where her father ministered as a pastor. Junior will inherit the contacts and friendships that I have with pastors of every continent, and his ministry will grow even greater than what we've reached today. When God uses him in the Word, he will have open doors around the world; all that he needs to do is remain faithful to what he has received freely. What my children have received is the fruit of much work, battle, labor, tiredness and perseverance. Parents teach God's Word to your children and go back to the family altar.

"Listen, my sons, to a father's instruction; pay attention and gain understanding. I give you sound learning, so do not forsake my teaching."

Proverbs 4:1-2 NIV

Teach in the Cities

Not only should it be our objective to teach our families the Scriptures, but our cities as well. *"They taught throughout Judah, taking with them the Book of the Law of the Lord; they went around to all the towns of Judah and taught the people"* (2 Chronicles 17:9 NIV).

The Bible says that king Jehoshaphat, son of Asa, charged his officials to go and teach the words of the Lord to the people. The big metropolises and capitals of the world need to hear the Word of God. For this reason we conduct evangelistic crusades around the world at the main centers and to the multitudes, because mass evangelism is very important and necessary. After every crusade, we leave a fruit of thousands of new believers, and churches grow and prosper under the direction and the strength of the Holy Spirit.

Leaders should receive the teaching of the Scripture and instruct others. Let's read what the book of Nehemiah teaches:

"On the second day of the month of the month, the heads of all the families, along with the priests and the Levites, gathered around Ezra the scribe to give attention to the words of the Law" (Nehemiah 8:13 NIV).

In actuality we are the priests of our family and we're responsible for the spiritual growth of it. We are the leadership along with other extraordinary leaders that have been equipped by God to teach the words of the Scripture. Paul said to Timothy: *"And the things you have heard me say in the presence of many witnesses entrust to reliable men who will also be qualified to teach others"* (2 Timothy 2:2 NIV). We need to learn by example of men of faith, and at the same time, teach with our example, attitudes, integrity and righteousness, in our private life, as well as ministry.

Teach in Church

We must teach the Church. Those in leadership are responsible for the training and instructing the Church with God's Word.

"It was he who gave some to be apostles, some to be prophets, some to be evangelists, and some to be pastors

and teachers, to prepare God's people for works of service, so that the body of Christ may be built up until we all reach unity in the faith and in the knowledge of the Son of God and become mature, attaining to the whole measure of the fullness of Christ. Then we will no longer be infants, tossed back and forth by the waves, and blown here and there by every wind of teaching and by the cunning and craftiness of men in their deceitful scheming. Instead, speaking the truth in love, we will in all things grow up [learning by instruction] into him who is the Head, that is, Christ. From him the whole body, joined and held together by every supporting ligament, [all of the ministries teaching in their specialized field] grows and builds itself up in love, as each part does its work."

Ephesians 4:11-16 NIV

We are responsible for equipping the Church of Jesus Christ with the principles of the Word with simplicity and the power of the Holy Spirit. In this manner we will build up a solid Church, mature, and capable of resisting the attacks of the enemy and remain standing in the midst of the spiritual battles, and overcome. Truly, the word of the prophet Isaiah has come to pass: *"Many peoples will come and say, 'Come, let us go up to the mountain of the LORD, to the house of the God of Jacob. He will teach us his ways, so that we may walk in his paths'. The law will go out from Zion, the word of the LORD from Jerusalem"* (Isaiah 2:3 NIV). The Church was founded on the day of Pentecost, in Jerusalem. Since then, it has taken God's Word to many towns and nations. From Zion came the Word of salvation, for the Bible declares the words of Jesus in the Gospel of John: *"for salvation is from the Jews"* (John 4:22b NIV).

Therefore, the first thing we must do is learn the Word, then teach it to our children, and to our cities; and as leaders, learn from one another. It is also our duty to instruct other leaders, and take these teachings to the churches so that they can mature and become strong in God's Word.

I would like to conclude this chapter sharing an experience with you. In 1986, during my stay in Istanbul, Turkey, I visited the Blue Mosque. In order to return to the hotel where I was staying I took a bus and I sat beside a young man. For the first time, someone was quicker than me to become social.

—You're a foreigner, aren't you? —He asked

To which I replied affirmatively. Then, fixing his eyes on me, he said:

—I want to invite you to convert to Islam. Would you like to become a Muslim?

I was surprised. This young man, I thought, is too good. I should be the one winning this friend to Christ...So I looked at him and said:

—Well, I would like to invite you to convert to Christ...

He smiled, and replied:

Shall we try to convert each other?

—OK, I replied. First you tell me about Islam, and then I will speak about Christ.

So he began:

—The Quran is the true word of God. The prophet Mohammed is the true prophet of God, and not Jesus Christ. He was a great man, and a prophet, but he is not God, for God couldn't have died on the cross.

He even spoke about the five pillars of the Islamic faith, etc... When he finished and perceived that it hadn't worked, he said:

—I'm done. Now you can speak.

I began by saying:

—Did you not know that the Quran was written six hundred years after the Bible and that your "true" book has hundreds of verses from my Bible? I received the Word before you received your original. And if the Bible came before the Quran, and the Quran contains many verses in my Bible, this means that you need to learn from me, and not me from you.

—I never heard anything like this before! He replied.

—Good, I said, then listen. You say that Jesus Christ was perfect, but He wasn't God. What you don't understand is that in order for you to be perfect you have to be God, because only God is perfect; this is where you err. To you the cross is a scandal. You are wrong again, because the message of the cross is foolishness to those who are perishing, but to us it's the power of God. And to finish I will ask you three questions. If you respond satisfactorily, I will convert to Islam right here, and now, and I will even change my name to Mohamed Ali.

—Then, ask them at once!, he said.

—First, I would like for Mohammed and Allah to forgive my sins.

-Sins! There is no sin.

—Well, your god is no good because Jesus forgave my sins. Second, I would like for the prophet Mohammed and Allah to give me the power of the Holy Spirit.

—Holy Spirit! I never heard of a Holy Spirit! He replied stunned.

—Well, your god is no good-I said- because I received the Holy Spirit, and He can give me power to live a righteous and holy life. Thirdly, I would like for the prophet

Mohammed and Allah to give me eternal life.

The young man exclaimed looking out the window and moving his hands:

—Eternal life? Nobody can give eternal life.

—Oh your god is really good for nothing- I affirmed. He can't forgive sins, he can't give me the power of the Holy Spirit, and he can't give me eternal life. What kind of god is he?

He remained silent, totally dazed. Then, looking at me getting ready to get off the bus, he said:

—I have nothing else to say.

—Oh, but I do! —I replied. Did you know that the prophet Mohammed had the opportunity to know Jesus, but he rejected Him? What about Mohammed's last words before he died, he said: "I have not found the truth yet!" But Jesus said: "I am the way, the truth, and the life"

(At this point, the young man was getting up from his seat to leave.) To finish the conversation I said:

—If I were to go with you to Mecca, in Saudi Arabia, the bones of the prophet Mohammed would be there. This is why there are guards watching over the tomb day and night, isn't that right?

—Oh, no! He replied. -Mohammed was taken to the heavens.

—O no! I said. He is in Mecca because if he weren't there then there would be no reason for the guards to watch over the tomb, right?

The young man remained silent, and perceiving that he was getting impatient, I concluded the conversation by saying:

—The difference between you and me is this: If I go with you to Mecca, we will find the bones of prophet Mohammed, but if you come with me to Israel, to the city of Jerusalem, you will see that Jesus' tomb is empty. His bones are not there because He has risen from the dead and He lives!

The young man's reaction immediately responded:

—I don't believe He has risen from the dead!

—O yes, I said. He is alive, and if you don't believe that he has risen, how can you then say that Mohammed was taken to the heavens?

After this discussion, there was no further answer... The young man got up, and got off the bus.

The Bible wins and will always win any argument that comes against it. It's the powerful Word of God. There is none like it. There is no "Sacred Book" that can resist the wisdom of the Scriptures. It is unique. It's a double-edged sword and cuts deep into the soul of any creature. All the founders of other cults and religions are dead, but Jesus Christ is alive. The Apostle Paul said to the Corinthian brothers:

> *Christ died for our sins according to the Scriptures,*
> *and that he was buried, that he was raised on the third*
> *day according to the Scriptures.*

1 Corinthians 15:3,4 NIV

He is alive; this is our hope and faith. We are different from everybody else, because we believe in a historic truth, and not a myth. We are unique and true. The Lord himself said in Revelation: *"I am the Living One; I was dead, and behold I am alive for ever and ever!"* (Revelation 1:18 NIV). Hallelujah! All glory be to His powerful name!

Chapter Six

The Bible Exhorts us Through its Words

In the presence of God and of Christ Jesus, who will judge the living and the dead, and in view of his appearing and his kingdom, I give you this charge: Preach the Word; be prepared in season and out of season; correct, rebuke and encourage — with great patience and careful instruction.

2 Timothy 4:1-2 NIV

When my daughter Kathryn began kinder garden, Junior was so excited to see his sister with a backpack and her school uniform, he was only three at the time, that he also wanted to go to school. Then we explained to him that he wasn't old enough to be admitted into school. However, our explanation didn't convince him. The following day, he got up very early only to see his sister Kathryn leave the house and get in the car with me to go to school. While he watched us drive away, Junior takes hold of Damaris' hand with one of his small hands, and with the other, waved at Kathryn with tears in his eyes.

Then, my wife and I began looking for a pre-school to send him, and we found a Christian one close to our house. Next, we went there and signed him up. This way he could learn to read and write and be instructed in God's Word as always, we did this regularly with our children at our family altar. You should have seen the joy in this child when we drove him to buy his backpack, pencils, drawing books, etc... He was so excited to study that his first day of class he got up at 5:45am, although classes began at 8:35am. The first day everything went fine. He didn't cry when we dropped him off at school. During that week and the following two weeks, he was "in the clouds". He rapidly got accustomed to classmates. But, when he learned that school was now mandatory, that he would have to get up early every morning, and learn to be responsible, he wanted to turn around and quit, because according to him, "he needed to sleep a little longer". His excitement didn't last too long. And I believe it's the same with all children, true?

At school, he learned many things, among them, the Word of God, which was taught in the proper fashion for children. After discussing the school issue with him, he changed his mind and continued going to school, but now with a greater enthusiasm. Every day he would learn a new Scripture, and along with Kathy he would play—preach in our living room, the "Kids Church services". Kathy would "sing", and he would "preach"; something like a minute or so, because the "preacher" didn't preach more than two minutes. One day, I went to school to pick him up, and getting in the car, Junior started telling me what he had learned during the day. So he asked me:

—Dad, do the angels of the Lord take care of me? Do they protect me?

—Well, of course son, I said.

Then he said:

—Then how is it that the Bible says that the angel of the Lord passed through Egypt at midnight and killed every firstborn child?

—Junior, what kind of question is this? — I asked. Then, I gave him a short explanation about the angels, and in the way they fulfill their responsibilities. There are angels for spiritual warfare, others that destroy cities, messengers, some that bring forth judgment from God, others that are ministers of the Lord for various purposes, others that worship God, those that help and protect us, etc... I did my best to explain it at his level of understanding. But it seemed like I didn't convince him much with my "explanation", because when we were arriving home, he looked at me and said:

—All right! I want the angels to take care of me every day when I go out, and go to school, but I don't want the Egyptian ones doing the job...OK?

Isn't this fun? Junior is as intelligent as Kathryn. Every day he comes up with questions that you wouldn't imagine. Not too long ago he wanted to get married! Kids...what an endowment from God it is to be parents, and what a gift are kids to us.

Preach the Word

"Preach the word; be prepared in season and out of season; correct, rebuke, and encourage"

2 Timothy 4:2 NIV

When the Lord instructs us by His Word, we have a great opportunity to grow spiritually. He always does it to our edification and never to our destruction. In a spur of anger someone can pressure and criticize another person in a destructive fashion, but God will never do that. He always desires our good and He will continually admonish us in a just and adequate manner. Let's read what the writer to the Hebrews declares: *"And you have forgotten that word of encouragement that addresses you as sons: 'My son, do not make light of the Lord's discipline, and do not lose heart when he rebukes you, because the Lord disciplines those he loves, and he* punishes everyone he accepts as a son.' Endure hardship as discipline; God is treating you as sons. For what son is not disciplined by his father?" (Hebrews 12:5-7 NIV). Therefore, God exhorts and admonishes us in different ways and in different situations, but always in the proper fashion, bringing the right word into each situation that will suit the purpose to edify our lives, and give us victory.

1 — Scripture exhorts us to learn the wisdom and instruction in God's Word

At that time Jesus went through the grain fields on the Sabbath. His disciples were hungry and began to pick some heads of grain and eat them. When the Pharisees saw this, they said to him, *"Look, your disciples are doing what is unlawful on the Sabbath"*. *He answered, "Haven't you read what David did when he and his companions were hungry? Or haven't you read in the Law...?"* (Matthew 12:1-3,5 NIV).

Jesus asked the critic Pharisees *"Haven't you read?"* The Bible teaches that we should read its words, for the purpose of learning its wisdom and teachings. Not understanding the Scriptures is always dangerous. The Pharisees knew all about Scripture, however, they lacked the understanding of the Spirit, and therefore, they were unable to acknowledge who the Lord Jesus really was. If we don't read the Scripture, we will not have the right mentality to understand God will or the wisdom contained in Scriptures. On a different occasion, the Pharisees, tried to find Jesus at fault asking Him: *"Some Pharisees came to him to test him. They asked, is it lawful for a man to divorce his wife for any and every reason? 'Haven't you read,' he replied, "that at the beginning the Creator made them male and female"* (Matthew 19:3-4 NIV). Notice that, one more time, Jesus asks the Pharisees: *"Haven't you read?"* In order for you to understand the basics of Scripture, you must read it. In order to understand God's wisdom, we must first read and apply its principles in our daily life. If we don't read it, we won't know was it has to say to us. When a child goes to school, he or she has the intent to learn how to read and write. In the same way, when someone comes to Christ, he or she begins to read and learn the Scripture; its writings will give each person the base or the foundation for their spiritual growth. How much time do you spend reading the Scripture? Do you dedicate a daily portion of your day to it?

The Lord Jesus teaches us the danger of not knowing the Scriptures: *"Jesus replied, 'You are in error because you do not know the Scriptures or the power of God'"* (Matthew 22:29 NIV).

You are in error! How many doctrinal errors, cults, and false religious groups have been birthed out of those who ignore Scripture? How many churches have fallen into grave doctrinal errors? How many leaders have mistaken with their congregations? How many members have followed the deception of various teaching, for the simple fact of not understanding the Scriptures? You may ask yourself: "Leaders?" Yes, leaders! Let's look at the two disciples on the way to Emmaus: *"He said to them, "How foolish you are, and how slow of heart to believe all that the prophets have spoken! Did not the Christ have to suffer these things and then enter his glory? And beginning with Moses and all the Prophets, he explained to them what was said in all the Scriptures concerning himself"* (Luke 24:25-27 NIV). These two men knew the Scriptures. They were His disciples; however, they did not understand what the Scriptures said concerning His resurrection. That's why they were walking sad and defeated. Then in verse 32 we read: "They asked each other, "Were not our hearts burning within us while he talked with us on the road and opened the Scriptures to us?" Here is the secret. Jesus opened their understanding so they could understand what the Scriptures said. Peter and John neither knew the Word of God in regards to Christ's resurrection: "They still hadn't understood that, according to Scripture, it was necessary that He rose from the dead". The disciples walked with Christ, they were with Him, saw His miracles and His power, they were instructed by the Lord during three and a half years, but they still did not reach the point of understanding the Scriptures in the proper fashion in regards to the resurrection. What will it be of us? We haven't seen Him; we only believe in Him and in His power. How will we know Him? —Through the Scriptures.

One time, a preacher was emphasizing that "David" prayed three times a day. The pastor, who was sitting at the platform thought he must have heard wrong and waited for the following sentence of the guest speaker; again he said: "David prayed three times a day..." The pastor whispered to him: "It's Daniel brother, Daniel..." But he could not hear the pastor because of his loud preaching and the shouting of the congregation. The young preacher continued saying that those jealous men went to the king and formulated a law for "David" to fall in their trap, but "David" continued praying three times a day... Then they took "David" y threw him into the lions den and... At this point, a brother stood up and said: "That's not David, brother, it's Daniel". But it was too late, for the preached had already thrown poor David into the lion's den. When he realized he was mistaken and, trying to fix his mistake, he looked at the pastor and then to the congregation and said with his arms extended sideways: "David, come out of there, my king. That is Daniel's place, the lions will eat you, come out..."

It's funny, but sad at the same time. Probably this preacher swapped Daniel for David because the names are similar in the first two letters. Or maybe he was really convinced that it was David and not Daniel. We don't know. The fact is we need to be careful with these things and be more knowledgeable of the Scriptures, to avoid this from happening. During the discourse at Pisidian Antioch, Paul emphasized in the prophecies for the purpose of bringing the Jews into the message of salvation through the Word. In the book of Acts, the Apostle Paul declared: *"Brothers, children of Abraham, and you God fearing Gentiles, it is to us that this message of salvation has been sent. The people of Jerusalem and their rulers did not recognize Jesus, yet in condemning him they fulfilled the words of the prophets that are read every Sabbath"* (Acts 13:26—27 NIV). Paul was truly an extraordinary preacher and well versed in the Scripture. He said to the Jews that the Word had been sent for them and that the reason they rejected Christ was that they did not comprehend the Scriptures that were read in their synagogues every Sabbath. The written word without discernment is comparable to spiritual death. The written word with discernment is comparable to revival and spiritual growth that daily unfolds inside our spirit—man through the reading of the Bible.

Paul, speaking of the Jews in his second letter to the Corinthians says: *"Even to this day when Moses is read, a veil covers their hearts. But whenever anyone turns to the Lord, the veil is taken away"* (2 Corinthians 3:15-16 NIV). Paul insisted in affirming that when the Law of Moses (the Pentateuch, the five books that Moses wrote, the Torah) is read, because of their ignorance of Scripture with regards to

Christ, and for not accepting Him as the Mesiah, they are not able to understand what they say. All the prophets have spoken about Christ and His coming to the world. Like Isaiah, for example, speaks to us about Jesus in chapter 53 of his book. Jesus himself declared that the leaders of His time did not receive Him because they ignored the Scriptures. Let's read what Jesus says in the Gospel of John: *"...nor does his word dwell in you, for you do not believe the one he sent. You diligently study the Scriptures because you think that by them you possess eternal life. These are the Scriptures that testify about me...but do not think I will accuse you before the Father. Your accuser is Moses, on whom your hopes are set. If you believed Moses, you would believe me, for he wrote about me. But since you do not believe what he wrote, how are you going to believe what I say?"* (John 5:38-39, 45-47 NIV)

Jesus clearly stated to the Jews of His days and even to us today, that if His Word does not abide in us; we cannot know Him. And if we truly search the Scripture, it will lead us to eternal life. It will help us understand about the Messiah from Genesis to Malachi, and it will reveal Jesus as the fulfillment of that which was accurately written. The Gospels testify of the Scripture's veracity showing us that Jesus fulfilled what was written of Him. From Acts to Revelation, we read the glorious mention of Jesus' marvelous Name. It exhorts us to know Him and allow Him to be the Lord of our lives. If you are reading about Messianic salvation and have not yet surrendered your heart to Jesus, do it right now. He will give you eternal life and will write your name in the Book of Life, and you will spend eternity by His side. Where else can you go? No religion can ever offer you what Jesus can offer you.

Some time ago a detailed and systematic research was conducted at a certain city, to find out how much people really know about the Scriptures. Many churches sent their representatives totaling a total of two hundred twenty-seven people. The group came to the test on the appointed day, and the professors formulated ten very easy questions from the Bible. These were the questions:

How many books are in the Bible? How many books in the Old Testament and how many in the New Testament?

When did Paul's conversion take place? Before or after His resurrection?

What was Christ's nationality?

Where do we find in the Bible the parable of the prodigal son? In the Old or New Testament?

What is the first book of the Bible ever written?

When was the Old Testament written? Before or after Christ?

How many Gospels are there in the Bible and where do you find them? In the Old or New Testament?

Write a name of a King of Israel, and if possible say how many years he reigned.

Write the name of one of Christ' disciples.

After how many days did Christ rise again?

The results of this small quiz were as follows: out of the two hundred and twenty-seven people that did the quiz, only twelve answered correctly the ten questions. The result of the two hundred and fifteen remaining people were as follows: eighteen of them did not know how many books were in the Bible, much less how many book there are in the Old and New Testament. Thirty people said that Paul's conversion occurred before Christ' resurrection. Thirty-one people did not know what Christ' nationality was, four said that he was a Greek and some other four said that His nationality was "Nazarene". Thirty-four people answered that the parable of the prodigal son was in the Old Testament. Eight could not tell what the first book of the Bible was. Twenty-five people said that the Old Testament was written after Christ. Two did not know how many Gospels existed, one person said they were in the Old Testament. Thirty-five people were not able to name a king of Israel and much less state how many years he reigned. Nebuchadnezzar and Pharaoh were named as kings of Israel. Twenty-seven people were not able to name one of Christ' disciples. Elijah and Elisha were identified as his two disciples. Five people did not know how many days after Christ' death, He resurrected.

What a sad condition! This is the reality in many of our churches. We place too much emphasis in programs and activities that do not edify the people, and these are the results. These two hundred twenty-seven people were sent by their local churches as representatives for the test, the "best" people they had. Just imagine in what condition the rest of the members of those congregations are! It is a shame that these results were found in "Evangelical Christian" congregations. We need to return to the Scriptures, to the knowledge and the wisdom in its pages.

2 — The Bible exhorts us to speak the message in God's Word

We are called to deliver the message contained in the Scripture. The preacher must not compromise the message, because of his denomination, supervisor, superintendent, or the president of his organization. He must deliver the message (whatever it may be) with boldness, courage and without fear. Remember what Paul said to Timothy: *"Preach the word...correct, rebuke and encourage"*. As ministers, we should not be impressed with the concepts of the "big speakers" of the denominations. Personally, I never allowed myself to be manipulated or impressed with the position of whoever it may be, even if I'm being observed while preaching. If I have to deliver a message, I will always do it with respect, in a kind and considerate fashion to those who are hearing it. I never quit preaching and being faithful to the truth, be it harsh, cutting and difficult to hear. Because the Word of God is like a sword that cuts, penetrates and produces conviction.

Let the prophet who has a dream tell his dream, but let the one who has my word speak it faithfully. For what has straw to do with grain? Declared the Lord, and like a hammer that breaks a rock in pieces?

Jeremiah 23:28-29 NIV

When we preach the message of the Word in truth, it produces awesome results. We are not here to please anyone. We have not been called of men, but of God, and He is the One who has given us the power and the anointing to speak His Word. *"Paul, an apostle —sent not from men nor by man, but by Jesus Christ and God the Father, who raised him from the dead."* (Galatians 1:1 NIV).

Paul is firm as to his position and calling to be an apostle. We must not be intimidated by the appearances of the "big" and "powerful"; much less to seek favors as some preachers do, to gain open doors for their ministries. During the crusades and conventions where I have preached, I perceived how many preachers run towards their "masters", always giving a pat on someone's back, to gain some kind of recognition. Sometimes I find these attitudes to be funny, however, in most of the cases I'm deeply concerned, how these "big guys", on the other hand, love to sit in front of everybody on the platform, occupying the first seats. The Lord himself rebukes us in regard to this sad reality:

> *Everything they do is done for men to see: They make their phylacteries wide and the tassels on their garments long; they love the place of honor at banquets and the most important seats in the synagogues; they love to be greeted in the marketplaces and to have men call them 'Rabbi' (master)*

Matthew 23:5-7 NIV

Paul also admonishes us about this same principle when writing the Galatians: *"Am I now trying to win the approval of men, or of God? Or am I trying to please men? If I were still trying to please men, I would not be a servant to Christ"* (Galatas 1:10 NIV). The Bible contains the message we must deliver; our responsibility is to preach it with courage, without fear or prejudice or felling intimidated by someone who is "greater" than us. Lets remember the Word of the Lord given to Jeremiah: "But the Lord said to me, *"Do not say, 'I am only a child.' You must go to everyone I send you to and say whatever I command you. Do not be afraid of them, for I am with you and will rescue you"*, declares the Lord" (Jeremiah 1:7—8 NIV).

Many leaders motivated by fear with the purpose of favoring certain groups, or by influence of their organizations, have compromised the truth that was entrusted to them to announce. They can no longer deliver the whole counsel of God, for they have compromised the Word in order to receive a favor. Many preachers can no longer speak against adultery, because they fear to suffer some kind of reprisal from their "masters" who have adulterat-

146

ed. In this manner, many for a lack of commitment and faithfulness to God's Word, remain in their positions untouched.

> *"Get yourself ready! Stand up and say to them whatever I command you. Do not be terrified by them, or I will terrify you before them. Today I have made you a fortified city, an iron pillar and a bronze wall to stand against the whole land —against the kings of Judah, its officials, its priests and the people of the land. They will fight against you but will not overcome you, for I am with you and will rescue you," declares the Lord"*

Jeremiah 1:17-19 NIV

God raised the prophet Jeremiah to preach the Word just as it is. The Lord knew that the leaders of Israel were out of line of His perfect will and far from His ways because of their personal interests. The kings, princes and priests represent the Church's leadership, those who are invested with authority, the ones who have been called to lead God's people. Unfortunately, some people motivated by self-interest benefit themselves with their "high" positions; they abandoned righteousness, integrity and their godly fear. They started right but they ended very wrong. Others, with wrong motivations totally backslid and acquired a wrongful and deceitful theology of prosperity. But thanks be to God that there are still men full of God's power, faithful leaders, men of honor, transparent, that are leading God's people with wisdom, respect and integrity. I know both sides of the coin; I've seen around the world both sides of leadership and have learned much from observing.

> *"This is the word that came to Jeremiah from the Lord: "Listen to the terms of this covenant and tell them*

to the people of Judah and to those who live in Jerusalem.
Tell them that this is what the Lord, the God of Israel
says: 'Cursed is the man who does not obey the terms of
this covenant…"

Jeremiah 11:1-3 NIV

In the book of the prophet Jeremiah, starting at verse 18 in chapter 11, it tells us about a "leadership" conspiracy against Jeremiah. And even today there still are leaders that conspire against true preachers of God's Word, closing doors, and using false and dishonest words against them in front of their colleagues, so that these true men of God don't have an opportunity to preach at their conventions and events. They go through all this trouble because they cannot stand when genuine preachers of the Gospel proclaim the truth. They fear that their evil deeds will be revealed and they will loose their positions. This is how they carry out their private agenda using a holy cause. Let's read what God says through the prophet: *"You must speak my words to them, whether they listen or fail to listen, for they are rebellious"* (Ezequiel 2:7 NIV).

We are called to proclaim the truth. If they do not want to hear it, its unfortunate, but we are not going to change our preaching style and our convictions just because they want us to. A conviction is not to be sold to receive a benefit; it is not to be exchanged for a favor or to receive an invitation. We should never compromise the truth to reach an "important position". The conviction of a believer or a preacher in God's Word is one of the most power weapons he or she can possess. Dear brother, be faithful to your calling. God has not given us a spirit of fear, but of power. Glorify Christ through the preaching of His Word!

Our calling is from God and His Spirit. *"Son of man, I have made you a watchman for the house of Israel; so hear the word I speak and give them warning for me"* (Ezekiel 3:17 NIV). He is the one who has calls, equips, supplies and supports. It's God! The gifting comes from God, the power is of God, our life belongs to Him; nothing is ours.

> *"But during the night an angel of the Lord opened the doors of the jail and brought them out. 'Go, stand in the temple courts,' he said, and tell the people the full message of the new life"*

Acts 5:19-20 NIV

We have the book, now we have to tell the "full" message of the life in Jesus Christ. The Bible encourages us to proclaim the message written in it. What a privilege it is to be called to preach His blessed Word! Paul, counseling Titus, encourages him to preach the message of the cross just as it is. *"These, then, are the things your should teach. Encourage and rebuke with all authority. Do not let anyone despise you"* (Titus 2:15 NIV). There is nothing more beautiful than to see an altar crowded with souls, after hearing the call, saved, happy, full of joy and contentment for receiving Christ. Paul encouraged Timothy: *"Do your best to present yourself to God as one approved, a workman who does not need to be ashamed and who correctly handles the word of truth"* (2 Timothy 2:15 NIV).

In the message that I preached to the pastors in the city of Kristiansand, Norway, in August of 1998, I said: "For us as ministers of God, there is nothing more extraordinary then to hear another preacher deliver a sermon following a train of thought in his introduction, body and conclusion. A man of truth, integrity, wisdom, and well versed in the knowledge of the Scriptures. Instructed in homiletics and hermeneutics, full of power and authority, and above all, humble to recognize that his ministry belongs to God and that the Lord uses him not for his ability of speech or because of his theological studies…"

One time, a very wise woman gave a word to her husband, a minister and preacher of the Gospel: "When you take the pulpit, place yourself in a position where everyone can see you, preach the message with power and authority so that everyone will respect you, and be short so that everyone will love you…" In the Book of Acts, we read that the preacher's of the New Testament Church prayed in times of persecution: *"Now, Lord, consider their threats and enable your servants to speak your word with great boldness. Stretch out your hand to heal and perform miraculous signs and wonders through the name of your holy servant Jesus. After they prayed, the place where they were meeting was shaken. And they were all filled with the Holy Spirit, and spoke the word of God boldly"* (Acts 4:29-31 NIV). Just as the brothers of the New Testament, we must boldly deliver the message of the Gospel. In this fashion we must announce the wonderful message of God's salvation, conscientious that *"If God is for us, who can be against us?"* (Romans 8:32 NIV).

In 1993, God showed Damaris and me the reason that Kathryn and Junior were sick. He opened our understanding to expose to the whole world the evils contained in the Disney videos. The movies contain subliminal pornographic messages, witchcraft, sorcery, astrology, violence; effeminate characters, immorality that goes against true family values, sponsor the New Age movement, subtle Satanic messages, inspiring the children to disobey their parents and many other things that we will not deal with in this book (if you as a reader desire to learn more about the Disney influence, you can obtain the videos from our ministry in which I explain about it in more detail). At that time, we understood that God had called us to raise our voice against this propaganda of evil. The Lord gave us boldness and courage to do it. We preached without fear or dread of anyone because we can prove what we say through many proofs. Thousands upon thousands of families and children around the world have been saved, restored and completely healed of all the evil influences of Disney and its products. We have received hundreds of letters, phone calls, e-mails, faxes and many thank you notes from people and families who now understand the reason for their children's violent behavior, who after hearing and obeying the Word of God where transformed. The Word that God gave us when He revealed this subject to us is in Deuteronomy: *"Do not bring a detestable thing into your house or you, like it, will be set apart for destruction. Utterly abhor and detest it, for it is set apart for destruction"* (*Deuteronomy 7:26 NIV*).

Surely many people oppose what we said about Disney, however, with all respect to them, I would say that their understanding is clouded and closed out to the working of the Spirit of God. If we have no air to breathe we die, and in the same fashion, without the discernment of the Spirit we are spiritually dead. Such persons have no maturity or discernment to see beyond what their human eye can see. Yes, pastors have also criticized us when we spoke against Disney. If we had no critics we would not be doing the work of God. If our Lord was criticized what would be of us? Thanks be to God, they are only "small group", because wherever we have gone, all over the world, thousands upon thousands of people have testified of how our message has blessed their lives, with peace, harmony and joy in their homes. Many criticize us because they envy the anointing and authority that God has given us. They contradict what we say about Disney because they don't have the courage and the boldness that God has given us by His Spirit. In this cowardly manner, at our backs, they, "blaspheme" against our ministry, receiving condemnation upon themselves, their families, just as Jesus said:

> *"But I tell you that men will have to give account on the day of judgment for every careless word they have spoken. For by your words you will be acquitted, and by your words you will be condemned"*

Matthew 12:36-37 NIV

3 — The Bible exhorts us to consider the pureness God's Word

One time Abraham Lincoln said: "The greatest gift that God gave man is the Bible and the purity of its words"

> *"And the words of the Lord are flawless, like silver refined in a furnace of clay, purified seven times".*

Psalm 12:6 NIV

If God is pure and holy, and He is the author of Scripture, the words of the Holy Bible are pure and holy as well. One day, Damaris and I felt it would be important to talk with Kathryn about some changes that she would undergo en her adolescence. She looked at us with the innocent look of a little girl of only nine years old. Holding her doll on her lap, feeding her "baby" the bottle, she listened to us attentively. At that point I perceived how precious the ministry of the Word worked in Kathryn's life. Her countenance transmits the innocence and holiness that's in her heart. Looking at her, my eyes began to well up in tears, and said: "Kathy, you are so innocent, my dear daughter..." She replied: "Of course daddy, I haven't committed a crime." Isn't wonderful when we teach our children the Word of God, and it works in their hearts, making them holy in their attitudes, gestures, words and actions?

"...The word of the Lord is flawless..."

Psalm 18:30b NIV

During the nineteenth century, there was a group of Christians, who for their ethics and integrity profoundly left a mark in their time, promoting great revivals in many cities. The Puritans, seen by some as a group of Presbyterian sectarians that interpreted the Scripture with seriousness and rigor, lived in holiness and righteousness before God. The Puritan Pastors conducted their ministry transparently and above reproach. Jonathan Edwards, the great puritan preacher and revivalist of New England, said one time: "A holy man is a powerful weapon in the hands of God". The men that have been used most by God in the past, and those today, are holy individuals in their personal life and in their ministries. If we are called to preach the Word of God, which is pure, we should also be pure, because we are the bearers of that Word. In 1875, a friend of D.L. Moody said to him: "Moody, God is searching for a man. Just one. Someone that is holy and totally consecrated to Him. Then, God will change the world through his life". To which Moody answered: "I will be that man!" Here's the secret. Holiness reveals God's character in us. If we truly desire revival we need to return to the moral principles of these men from the past. God can use us today in the same way He used these men in the past. God is the same; we are the ones that change. One time, John Wesley declared: "Give me a hundred preachers that don't fear anyone, but God, holy men that reject sin, and desire nothing but God, and they will change the world for Christ". This is the path. The Word of God purifies our life turning us into men and women equipped to serve God.

> *"The precepts of the Lord are right, giving joy to the heart. The commands of the Lord are radiant, giving light to the eyes"*

Psalm 19:8 NIV

If we desire to have discernment and our "spiritual eye" illuminated, we must keep the precepts and the commands of God's Word in our heart. After David committed adultery with Bathsheba and the prophet Nathan came to him, David declared: *"...So that you are proved right when you speak and justified when you judge"* (Psalm 51:4 NIV). The Word of God is just and pure, there is no impureness or contamination in it. *"Your promises have been thoroughly tested, and your servant loves them"* A different translation reads: *"Thy word is very pure"* (Psalm 119:140). Another version says: *"Your word is very pure"*. The purity of God's Word makes us holy and equips us to serve Him. The Apostle Paul, writing to the Ephesians teaches us that Christ showed His love for the Church purifying it with His Word: *"...just as Christ loved the church and gave himself up for her to make her holy, cleansing her by the washing with water through the word"* (Ephesians 5:25-26 NIV).

4 — The Bible Exhorts us to See the Perfection in God's Word

> *"The law of the Lord is perfect, reviving the soul, the statutes of the Lord are trustworthy, making wise the simple"*

Psalm 19:7 NIV

154

The Word is perfect, and so are its commandments. The quality of God's Word is intimately related to God's character, completely flawless. All of its contents are spiritual. Its words are the highest expression of ethics and perfection. The Word compiles all the conceivable qualities, reaching the highest degree in a scale of values. The Word is excellent, and has been given to men in the best imaginable form. God is the great author. From the ten-commandments that were written in the tablets of the law, to the epistles written by the Apostles, all Scripture was inspired and revealed by God, and God being perfect, so are His Words. *"So then, the law is holy, and the commandment is holy, righteous and good"* (Romans 7:12 NIV).

The holiness, perfection and the righteousness of the Word are the fruits of God's holy, perfect and righteous character. The book of Psalms also declares: *"As for God, his way is perfect"* (Psalm 18:30 NIV). How does He teach us His Word? Through His perfect Work.

> *Whether you turn to the right or to the left, your ears will hear a voice behind you, saying, "This is the way; walk in it".*
>
> Isaiah 30:21 NIV

This is the way. When Isaiah prophesized that John the Baptist would prepare the way for the coming of the holy and perfect Son of God, he said: *"A voice of one calling: In the desert prepare the way for the Lord; make straight in the wilderness a highway for our God"* (Isaiah 40:3 NIV). Jesus was holy and perfect. He always stated the authenticity of the Scriptures, referring to the words of the prophets as the Word of God. He himself is the fulfillment of the Word.

In Psalm 119 is the classic expression of the Word in

every aspect. When you meditate in the words of those 176 verses, you will read what the Word of God truly is. He will never fail. We are the only ones who can err. Sometimes we can lurk in failure for the simple reason of not knowing His Word, and we embrace failure as the will of God.

One time a man bought a ticket on a luxury cruise liner. His money was enough to buy the ticket, but he didn't have enough money to buy meals on-board the ship. So he took some sandwiches that lasted only for one day of his journey. On the second day, he had no more food and he didn't eat for the remaining three days. While he walked around the ship, he watched how people walked in and out of the ship's restaurant. When he walked up to the restaurant's entrance, he was starving, he wanted to eat the leftovers of the other passengers, or do some work in exchange for food. Suddenly, a man dressed as a waiter came out through the restaurant's entrance, the man starving and desperate, approached him, and asked: "Excuse me, please listen to me! I'm starving and it's been several days since I haven't had a meal. I'll do what you ask me to do, as long as I can get some food."

The young man, surprised by his request asked him: "Can I see your ticket, please". Immediately, the man pulled out the ticket from his pocket and showing it to the waiter, he said:

—Here it is!

The young man, startled by what he was hearing, said to the man:

—You have not eaten out of ignorance.

—What do you mean? The man asked.

The young man replied:

—Look here. It says that the bearer of this ticket is

entitled to make use of every service onboard the ship. This includes: playrooms, cinemas, the club, the restaurant, etc... And looking at the man completely astounded, the waiter concluded saying: "You have not eaten, for the simple reason that you did not read the fine print on your ticket"

My dear brother and sister, it's always our mistake! On Calvary's cross Jesus bought our ticket to eternal life. He redeemed us from our sin and has seated us with Him in high places. Many Christians don't enjoy of the immeasurable riches of Christ because they haven't read their rights and privileges in the Scripture. Everything is on the ticket: The Bible. In the Word, God's promises that lead us to our victory are written for our benefit. Satan has sustained his victory in the life of many believers that live sick and tormented simply because they haven't read the promises written on the ticket, they haven't read the pages of the Bible about healing in the Name of Christ and the power of the blood.

No Limits

David said that as hard as a man tries to reach perfection in anything he does, he would always be limited. But the Word of God is unlimited, it has no end, it's not subject to natural law, which is limited because it only applies to the realm of what is human and fallible. God's Word is perfect, infinite, and indestructible and has survived the most furious attacks of the men that have come against it.

"To all perfection I see a limit; but your commands are boundless"

Psalm 119:96 NIV

It has also resisted the test of time because, to this day, after thousands of years, God's Word, the Bible, is still in our hands and will be with us forever. It also sanctifies us. Sanctification is a process, but holiness is a state. Day by day we are perfected, and made holy by the effect of God's Word and by what we have applied of it in our lives. We are changed from glory to glory, until we reach perfect holiness in Jesus Christ, then we go to live with Him forever. Let's remember Paul's exhortation: *"Being confident of this, that he who began a good work in you will carry it on to completion until the day of Christ Jesus"* (Philippians 1:6 NIV).

The psalmist declares: "As for God, his way is perfect; the word of the Lord is flawless." The Word is perfect, because something without impurities is perfect, like refined gold that is cleaned of all impurities. If we desire to walk in God's righteous ways, we must place His words as a lamp unto our feet, and He will perfect our ways. *"It is God who arms me with strength and makes my way perfect"* (Psalm 18:32 NIV). Do you want to walk in the right path? Walk in accord with God's Word. It will sanctify and perfect the path you must walk in. Our transformation is done by the Spirit of God, transforming our thought patterns in accord to what God would have in our lives. The Lord desires that in every realm of our life we walk according to His pleasing will, which is always perfect and good. This is what the apostle Paul says to us when he wrote to the Romans: *"Do not conform any longer to the pattern of this world, but be transformed by the renewing of your mind. Then you will be able to test and approve what God's will is —his good, pleasing and perfect will"* (Romans 12:2 NIV). Do you want to know what your calling is? Do you want to know where you will serve the Lord? Do you want to know God's will for your life regarding marriage? Then seek His direction for every realm of your life, and all things will go well for you.

Let's read what James teaches in his letter: *"But the man who looks intently into the perfect law that gives freedom, and continues to do this, not forgetting what he has heard, but doing it —he will be blessed in what he does"* (James 1:25 NIV). We will know God's perfect will, when we learn His perfect Word. It's very simple! The secret is to walk in His ways.

5 — The Bible Teaches us to Keep its Words

To keep something is having a protective attitude. We are on the vigil, like a watchman, protecting that which we love. Just as a bodyguard will defend the person he is guarding, we must guard and defend what God has given us. We preserve and safeguard the most sacred things that we have, God, our family, ministry and friends. Milton Nascimiento, in spite of not knowing God, said something very true in one of his songs: "A friend is something to safeguard under seven keys, on the left side of our chest, inside the heart…" We all safeguard precious memories, and lovingly treasure the happy moments that we spend next to our true friends that to this day have been faithful. We preserve in our mind the memory of the love that our parents showed throughout our life. We keep the happy thoughts of our marriage and the birth of our children. To this day, I remember the time I was at the hospital room, with my wife, when she delivered each one of our children (Kathryn and Junior). I hold precious memories of fellow ministers that helped in the past and still help us today with their words of wisdom. Finally, we all remember with great joy the day we surrendered our live to Christ. Our mind stores the times we spent with Him; when God worked extraordinary miracles in our lives. Tears of joy roll down our cheeks when we recall the wonderful experiences that show us His faithfulness, protection and provision for our lives. Paul counseled Timothy, his son in the faith: *"I charge you, in the sight of God and Christ Jesus and the elect angels, to keep these instructions"* (1 Timothy 5:21 NIV). He even increases the level of responsibility of his disciple, when he advises him: *"Timothy, guard what has been entrusted to your care"* (1 Timothy 6:20 NIV). Paul speaking of himself, expressing his hope in Christ, said: *"...I am convinced that he is able to guard what I have entrusted to him for that day"* (2 Timothy 1:12 NIV). We have a deposit in a heavenly bank that no one can steal. Therefore, we must keep the Word in our hearts; that's our job. Jesus said we must keep the Word: *"Behold, I am coming soon! Blessed is he who keeps the words of the prophecy in this book"* (Revelation 22:7 NIV). Keep His Word in your heart with esteem. Solomon the sage said: *"Discretion will protect you, and understanding will guard you"* (Proverbs 2:11 NIV), and he adds: *"...blessed is he who keeps the law..."* (Proverbs 29:18); happy, prosperous, full of joy, peace, cheerfulness and contentment.

The Word of God must be kept

With strength

> *"Be very strong; be careful to obey all that is written in the Book of the Law of Moses, without turning aside to the right or to the left".*

> Joshua 23:6

We are accustomed to guard the things that are valuable to us; but above these things, we should treasure God's Word because Christ is the revelation of God the Father. He remains forever above all things. We should keep in our heart the Words of His testimony.

With Understanding

> *"May the Lord give you discretion and understanding when he puts you in command over Israel, so that you may keep the law of the Lord your God".*

1 Chronicles 22:12

Understanding is the capacity to comprehend, realize or figure out something about a matter. As His children we need to comprehend what our Father wants us to understand by the judgments He has established in His Word.

With Discernment

> *"He who keeps the law is a discerning son..."*

Proverbs 28:7

A discerning man who keeps the Word is wise, he will act with understanding, he will try to avoid all the things he considers to be wrong or that will produce harm. He will be a doer of good deeds and will be careful to do things right. A man that walks cautiously in his way and watchfully in his tasks; he's always alert to the attacks from the enemy of his soul. He prepares in every ethical conduct of the Word, he keeps himself of everything and everybody.

With Faith

> *"...For he guards the lives of his faithful ones and delivers them from the hand of the wicked..."*

Psalm 97:10

If we keep the Word, it will guard us. The benefit of keeping the Word is reciprocal: You keep the Word, God keeps you. In the difficult moments of life, the Word will keep you and give you victory. If you keep it and trust it, the Lord will always be at your side.

> *"See, I am sending an angel ahead of you to guard you along the way and to bring you to the place I have prepared. Pay attention to him and listen to what he says...I will be an enemy to your enemies..."*
>
> Exodus 23:20-22

The Scriptures are full of divine protection promises. In the priests blessing, in the book of Numbers we read: *"The Lord bless you and keep you"* (Numbers 6:24). In Hannah's prayer, we read: *"He will guard the feet of his saints"* (1 Samuel 2:9). In the Book of Psalms we read: *"The Lord protects the simple hearted"* (Psalm 116:6), it also says: *"The Lord watches over all who love him"* (Psalm 145:20). If you love God, He will keep you safe anywhere, in any circumstance and facing any problem. If we are faithful and follow His principles, we will surely obtain the results of obedience.

During the 1960s, in the former Soviet Union, a young lady was preparing her thesis to be presented in Moscow. She was going to elaborate at a public debate, in front of an international audience that had been invited to hear what she had to say at the Kremlin about socialism, Marxism and Leninism. She would give her point of view, highlighting the defense of communism and atheism in front of people from various nations invited for that event. When this young lady was almost finishing her thesis in her grandfather's library, the clock was showing it to half past two in the morning. That same day she had to go to the Soviet Government Palace at ten in the morning to do her presentation. When she finished, she got up to relax a little and reduce mental fatigue. Walking by the library she began to pass her hand quickly over some of the books and to read some titles. Coincidentally, she found an old Bible that belonged to her grandfather who had been a pastor. Intrigued, she took to Bible off the shelf and opened it. To her surprise, she found a small piece of paper with a prayer written on it by her grandfather that said: "Oh, Lord, save all of my family. Deliver them and guard them from the lies of socialism and protect them from the falsehood of communism. Reveal your Word to my children and grandchildren and let them know You. In the power of Your Name, on my knees and with tears in my eyes, I pray, Almighty God, Amen! Suddenly, the Holy Spirit shook this young lady and filled her with conviction of sin. She remembered as a child how her grandfather placed her on his laps and opened that old Bible to teach her Bible stories. Immediately, the Spirit of God brought to her memory when some of her relatives died for the cause of Christ, for not denying the Lord. However, she had been trying to blot out of her memory these remembrances; she had given her back and rejected God and His Word. Then, falling on her knees, in profound conviction, she bitterly wept and asked the Lord to forgive her. Right then she gave her heart to Christ and received Him at about four o'clock in the morning. At ten o'clock, she was ready to give her speech about the Kremlin. When she began her speaking, to everyone's surprise she said: "This morning I will present my thesis and my defense...There has been a slight change...This morning, at four o'clock, I found my grandfather's old Bible and through it, I received the true sense of life which is Christ and His Word. I come to defend the thesis of a holy cause, about the Church of the Lord Jesus, and I declare that Marxism and Leninism and every socialist system are lies and deceits. I understand the consequences that my words will bring upon me this morning, but I am willing to leave it all, even to the point of having to face a concentration camp or a firing squad. As long as I have eternal life in Christ, I'm ready to die for God and His Word" Can you imagine how this surprised the soviet leaders and the international guests present there? God is wonderful! He used that unique opportunity to demonstrate the power of conviction in His Word and the power of prayer of a grandfather for her granddaughter. We do not know what happened to the young lady, but if they tortured and killed her, she is with Christ. It does not matter! She is safe in our Heavenly Father's hands. We should remember Peter's exhortation: *"...who through faith are shielded by God's power..."* (1 Peter 1:5). If this young lady remains alive in prison under a sentence for her behavior that put to shame a whole system in front of the international press and the guests, this Word is for her: *"Since you have kept my command to endure patiently, I will also keep you..."* (Revelation 3:10). In conclusion, when we keep His Word in strength, understanding, faith and discernment, He will also keep us in all our ways. This is His promise, and He will not fail. We are kept in Him, for Him and by Him. God in wonderful! Great is His power and His Word is unlimited. Wherever our ministerial team goes, anywhere in the world, I know that God is with us and that He will keep us in all of our ways because we work for Him and not for ourselves. Hallelujah! He is truthful, and his faithfulness goes beyond the heavens.

> *"...The one who was born of God keeps him safe, and the evil one cannot harm him..."*

1 John 5:18

6 — The Bible Exhorts us to Guard its Words in our Heart

When we study human anatomy we learn that the heart is a hallow organ, made of muscle tissue, located in the thorax, with two auricles and two ventricles that receive blood and pump it through by rhythmic movements. From a spiritual perspective, it is the center of our deepest intimate profound emotions and has the ability to love or hate. In our heart abide our attitudes, thoughts and actions, helping us to discern between good and evil. We can have a heart with God's characteristic or an evil heart, full of the characteristics of lowly passions, perversion and dishonesty, and uncleanness from the devil. Jesus said: *"The good man brings good things out of the good stored up in his heart, and the evil man brings evil things out of the evil stored up in his heart"* (Luke 6:45).

There are two realms: Good and evil. Paul speaking to the Romans about sexual immorality, speaks of those who practice deviant sexual activities with the same sex, and says: *"Therefore God gave them over in the sinful desires of their hearts to sexual impurity for the degrading of their bodies with one another"* (Romans 1:24). Their minds had become insensitive, there was no conviction of the Holy Spirit; they totally rejected salvation and degraded their bodies with one another. In the beginning God established marriage between a man and a woman, is not enough for these people. Paul says that these men's *"consciences have been seared as with a hot iron"* (1 Timothy 4:2). Such persons are not worthy of sympathy, because they have been deceived by the devil. I am not saying that they are bad individuals in the sense of getting along with others. What I am saying is that they have been possessed by an evil spirit in their hearts by disobeying a natural law that God established, thus committing an abomination in the sight of God and His Word.

"Because of this, God gave them over to shameful lusts. Even their women exchanged natural relations for unnatural ones. In the same way the men also abandoned natural relations with women and were inflamed with lust for one another. Men committed indecent acts with other men, and received in themselves the due penalty for their perversion."

Romans 1:26-27)

Paul goes on to say: *"Furthermore, since they did not think it worthwhile to retain the knowledge of God, he gave them over to a depraved mind, to do what ought not to be done"* (vs. 28). These people have rejected the knowledge of God's Word. We get to know God through His Word, there is no other way. Many of these men and women once knew God, but they backslid from the Lord's ways and their last state became worst than their first. We pray for them in Christian love, feeling sorrow for them, but believing that they will return to Christ in repentance, as many have done so leaving their shameful practices. Many accept and receive Christ around the world are assisted spiritually by others that have been in the same situation, but have been delivered, redeemed and forgiven by Christ. Nobody is born a homosexual; this is a lie from the devil. The person chooses to be one out of his own free will. However, if this person receives Christ: He will forgive him, his heart will be cleansed by the blood of the Lamb of God, and his soul shall be delivered from eternal damnation. Jeremiah, the prophet declares: *"The heart is deceitful..."* (Jeremiah 17:9). Because of its deceitfulness, the Bible teaches us to keep His Word in our heart. *"My son, do not forget my teaching, but keep my commands in your heart...* " (Proverbs 3:1). It is in the heart where the teachings of the Word must be kept. If we just do it mentally, we can be convinced in our intellect, but not in our spirit. The problem is that many people mentally know they are mistaken, but have no conviction of the Holy Spirit to forsake sin. *"Lay hold of my words with all your heart..."* (Proverbs 4:4).

God's Law Written in our Hearts

Solomon advises us to keep His Word with **"all"** of our heart. We must keep the Word of God in every realm of our life. We must never forget that Scripture should take the center of our hearts. *"I will put my law in their minds and write it on their hearts"* (Jeremiah 31:33). God has written on the inside of us His commandments. When we disobey His Word we have no excuse. We all have the power to choose between good and evil. Sin is a choice; you freely choose to sin against God's moral, spiritual and written Laws. God has written his laws in our heart; this is what the Scripture declares: Since they show that the requirements of the law are written on their hearts, their consciences also bearing witness, and their thoughts now accusing, now even defending them. (Romans 2:15) We all have a conscience, which is the voice of God in our heart. He has engraved His written law, the Bible. And, if this were not enough, He gave us a conscience (the voice of conviction); which is God's spiritual law. Our conscience is in our soul, where our intellect resides. Why has God's Divine Law set it to be this way? Paul declares in Romans: *"This will take place on the day when God will judge men's secrets through Jesus Christ, as my gospel declares"* (Romans 2:16). His moral law tells us what is right and what is wrong; through it, God leads us in the right path, therefore, men will have no excuse on judgment day.

Marilyn Laszlo had dedicated her entire life to the translation of the Bible for the Hauna people of New Guinea. One day, as she was translating, she came across the word "sin". So she began asking the Hauna people what they thought sin would be according to their culture.

Sin—said the Hauna people—is when we lie, steal, kill, and also when a man takes someone else' wife.

Laszlo was surprised. The Hauna people, in spite of not knowing God, they were speaking of God's model contained in the Law that God gave Moses on Mount Sinai: The Ten Commandments. There is no excuse! God has written His law inside of us. This shows us once more that the Bible is truly God's Word. The Lord will judge us by our actions.

Repentance and Conversion

The Apostle Paul, writing to the Christians in Rome, expressed to them how greatly he delighted in God's law. God's law works not only in our intellect but in our spirit as well. Someone can be convinced about something in the intellect but not in the spirit. It can be inside the mind but not in the heart. *"For in my inner being I delight in God's law"* (Romans 7:22).

The reason why so many people don't come to Christ is because they have never been reached in the most inner part of their being, only in their intellect. We are encouraged to love and serve the Lord with all of our being: *"Love the Lord your God with all your heart and with all your soul and with all your strength"* (Deuteronomy 6:5). We have a body (strength), a soul (mind), a spirit (heart). Just as God is triune, so are we. Let's read what the Apostle Paul says: *"May your whole spirit, soul and body be kept blameless at the coming of our Lord Jesus Christ"* (1 Thessalonians 5:23). God's judgment in our lives will be in three degrees. For this reason people have much difficulty understanding the differences between these three dimensions.

Many do not understand the difference between the mind and the spirit. For example, there are three levels of repentance. I will call the first level an "intellectual repentance". The person acknowledges his or her wrong doings and sinful state. The second one is an "emotional repentance". In hearing God's voice the person's emotions are deeply touched, as the psalmist said: *"I am troubled by my sin"* (Psalm 38:18). The third level would be a willful, true, and genuine repentance. The person confesses sin: *"...I will confess my transgressions to the Lord and your forgave the guilt of my sin"* (Psalm 32:5).

Then again, I consider there are five degrees of conversion. First, the *"mental conversion"*, which occurs when a person has a change of mind, view point, but does not believe or repent. Secondly, the *"political conversion"*, this occurs when a person adheres to a cause or a political ideology. Thirdly, would be a *"religious conversion"*, which occurs when the person becomes religious but is not saved. The person was inducted to a religion and not to the truth; therefore, there is no assurance of eternal life with Christ. In forth place, a *"moral conversion"*, which occurs when a person ceases to be considered a "bad" person in society; after having been accused of committing hideous crimes. This would only be an outward change. No prison system in the world can change a person's heart; only Christ can do it. Lastly, the fifth degree is *"true conversion"*, this takes place when a person's life changes radically and completely by accepting Christ as Lord and Savior; only then a true repentance of sin occurs by the conviction of the Holy Spirit wholly operating in the soul, emotions, intellect, spirit and body.

One time, a young lady insisted that she did not believe in God, however, she felt guilty for having sex with her boyfriend. How can this be? Guilt is the voice of conscience. It is something that God created so nobody can be excused on that Day. Instead of feeling remorse, she should repent and return to Christ. Remorse is not repentance it is a human emotion. Repentance is produced by the Spirit of God to lead a person to salvation. Judas, for example, did not repent for selling Jesus to the religious leaders; he had remorse that is why he hanged himself. If he would have repented, like Peter did, after denying the Lord, he would have been forgiven and restored just as Peter. See the difference?

> *Or do you show contempt for the riches of his kindness, tolerance and patience, not realizing that God's kindness leads you toward repentance? But because of your stubbornness and your unrepentant heart, you are storing up wrath against yourself for the day of God's wrath, when his righteous judgment will be revealed. God will give to each person according to what he has done.*

> Romans 2:4-6

A waitress

In the 1950's, when the Soviet Union was communist, a Bible smuggler lodged in a Moscow hotel. In prayer, the Lord instructed him to place a New Testament on the tray in which his meals where brought in. So, in a napkin, well hidden, he placed a New Testament, so that when the waitress came to take the tray she would unnoticeably take what was under the napkin. One of the ladies in house-keeping came to the room to carry out her regular room cleaning service, took the tray, and ten or fifteen minutes later, someone came knocking at the door. He thought: "O Lord! It's the KGB. Now what do I do?" To his surprise, when he opened the door, the hallway was full of hotel maids. The lady that had come for the tray said: "He only gave me a New Testament, in spite that every day one of us cleans his room. We are here to ask you for a copy of God's Word for each maid, we have been trying to get a New Testament with all of our hearts; and if you don't give us one, we will be very disappointed."

May God help us to put into practice what we have learned, and we will be blessed in everything we do. But if we disobey his precepts, nothing that we do will be prospered.

Chapter Seven

The Heathen, the Saved and their Relationship with God's Word

My wife as well as my sons can travel with me only in the summer, since it is their school vacation period. So every year we use that time to travel together. While I preach in the evangelistic crusades, they go out and have fun. Since they study all year it's right for them to enjoy some time off. My wife also uses that time to relax. She takes care of the kids and she helps them in their homework all the year during my absence, for that reason, she also needs some days to renew her strength. I also enjoy very much my family's presence after having been alone in so many trips. One year we had the opportunity of spending time alone together in Europe. We visited Spain, Italy, France, Great Britain, and Holland. We visited the city of Amsterdam, for Dr. Billy Graham invited me to participate in the International Evangelistic Conference together with ten thousand evangelists and itinerant ministers. From there we traveled to California, where we stayed just two days. Then, we continued to Japan and Tokyo for a great evangelistic crusade with Brazilians, Hispanics, Europeans, Philippines, and Japanese. For this event, we had the support of over eighty churches. In August 1998 we also went to Oslo and Christiansen in Norway. There, I preached in a crusade, and Damaris preached to the Norwegian and Hispanic women. One evening some children fro the church, together with my children Kathy and Junior, had come together to make up "an imitation of a church service" while we were eating dinner.

Kathy led "worship", and the kids were excited. Junior said "Oh, Kathy, I know all your songs." Then, Kathy turned the service over to Junior and said, "Now I turn the service over to the little preacher Josué Yrión Junior." One of the "small congregation" had the idea of recording Junior's" sermon." They looked for a tape and placed it in the recorder; the did a quick test to see if the recorder worked and recorded what the little, six-year-old "preacher", native of the states, had to say.

Junior calmly started his sermon and continued calmly. Then he began to raise his voice toward the "audience" , and said "Children, I would like to greet everyone in the name of Jesus, and…and…"His mind went blank, but he continued saying "and…my wife and my two children also greet you" they all started to laugh. Can you imagine? He is so small, and already with a wife and two kids. Afterward, he told me that he said that because that is the way I greet the church. But Junior did not loose his calmness and, also laughing, went on to say: "Today I will preach about Samson." When Kathy heard what the sermon was going to be about, she said "Oh, Junior, I know all your little sermons. Preach another because that one I already know by heart." But Junior did not loose his posture and went on with his sermon. "And Samson took a piece of bone in his hand and killed one million Philistines…" We, who were listening to the "great service" from the dining room, yelled "Junior! It was not a million, Samson killed a thousand Philistines." To what Junior replied: "It is the same for God to kill one thousand or one million. The power of God is the same." You can imagine the children's laughter and ours when we heard the "preacher." We were astonished as to how quickly he "fixed" the words of his "sermon" and adjusted them within his logical range, recognizing the glory, the power and the majesty of God. What perception of the child to state that for God to kill a million adversaries is the same as to kill a thousand! Praise be to God for Junior's life! In the future he will take my place in ministry and I believe that God will use him in a great way throughout the whole world.

One time, a philosopher asked: "If Plato and Jesus came to earth again, and both would be giving a discourse at the same time, in two different places, Which one would you like to hear?" And as he finished his speech, he stated: "Who would go to hear Plato speak about 'the truth' when instead, you could listen directly from Jesus' lips: *'I am the way, the truth, and the life'?*" (John 14:6) He is the truth! Jesus himself, praying to the Father, quoted God's Word saying, *"Your word is truth"* (John 17:17). There is no other Book like the Bible. The Bible itself proclaims to be the absolute truth. There is no work that deals with men's spiritual situations like the Bible does.

Job, in spite of his physical and emotional state, and in so much agony, said that he would never deny God's Word: *"Then I would still have this consolation—my joy in unrelenting pain—that I had not denied the words of the Holy One"* (Job 6:10).

Who would say that someone who had denied the Word had been able to escape the consequences? No one! *"The Lord announced the word, and great was the company of those who proclaimed it"* (Psalm 68:11).

Revival

When we observe and obey His Word we are always blessed. In every continent I have preach that there will be a world revival. How will it be? How will that revival come? What will be the force that will bring such movement? The revival will come through the power of God's Word. Let us pray as Habakkuk: *"Lord, I have heard of your fame, I stand in awe of your deeds, O Lord. Renew them in our day, in our time make them known"* (Habakkuk 3:2). God will bring the greatest outpouring of the power of the Holy Spirit that ever happened in history. It will be the last harvest of souls, where millions upon millions will convert to God. This is the revival that will come through the power of the Word of God:

> *"Look at the nations and watch and be utterly amazed. For I am going to do something in your days that you would not believe, even if you were told"*

Habakkuk 1:5

During our crusades in any part of the world, when participating in radio and television interviews, I always mention this verse of the book of Habakkuk. This verse inspires me in a very especial way because I believe and preach a revival. Jesus caused a revolution through his life and ministry during the Roman dominion of Israel. After the crucifixion and resurrection, the disciples of Emmaus declared something that lets us perceive with clarity the influence exerted through Jesus' ministry: *"He was a powerful prophet, powerful in word and deed before God and all the people"* (Luke 24:19).

The words of Christ caused a spiritual revival in Israel when many acknowledged and accepted him as the Messiah and as the answer to the prophecies of the Scriptures. Jesus himself referred to his own words in the following way: *"I tell you the truth, whoever hears my word and believes him who sent me has eternal life and will not be condemned; he has crossed over from death to life"* (John 5:24).

One time, Jesus asked his disciples if any of them wanted to depart, and they said, *"Lord, to whom shall we go? You have the words of eternal life"* (John 6:68). He alone has in his hands the ability to give eternal life, and eternal life comes only through his words; like He himself affirmed: *"If anyone keeps my word, he will never see death".*

His words are the only guarantee we have in relation to the eternal destiny of our souls. In the priestly prayer, Christ thanks the Father for his disciples who had believed in him, and he said: *"They were yours; you gave them to me and they have obeyed your word"* (John 17:6).

A young man that studied in a Theological Seminar invited his classmates to play basketball. They went to the gymnasium of a public school that was located near the seminar. The man that took care of the school allowed these young men to play while he patiently waited until they finished. He was a black, elderly man with white hair, who while he waited, he sat to read his old Bible. One day, one of the young men came near to him and asked him, "What are you reading?"

He answered," I am reading the book of Revelation."

A little surprised, the young seminar student asked again, "But, do you understand this book?"

The old man answered, "Of course I do, young man."

"And do you understand the meaning of the book of Revelation?", the young man asked again.

With great friendliness and calmness the old man replied, "That Christ is the victor!"

The Growth of the Church

Concluding, let us be sure that we know that the Bible

in all its books affirms that Christ is victorious. If He is victorious, the Word is victorious, because Christ is the Word of God. The Primitive Church grew extraordinarily because it believed that Christ was the victor (Acts 6:7). The Bible declares that the growth of the Primitive church was surprising because the Word of God was preached with power and authority, and because Christ was victorious: *"But the Word of God continued to increase and spread"* (Acts 12:24). The Church grew in miracles, in power, in wonders, in anointing, and victory with the proclamation of the Gospel. The membership of the Church was multiplied overwhelmingly. Here is the secret for the pastors that wish that their churches would grow. If you are a minister of God that desires to see the growth of your flock, preach the Word like it is, and you will obtain incredible results in your life, family, ministry and church.

The disposition of the disciples and of the leaders of the Primitive Church was so great that, regarding to Paul and his helpers, we read in the Scriptures that: *"all the Jews and Greeks who lived in the province of Asia heard the word of the Lord"* (Acts 19:10). That is more than extraordinary! They preached in all of Asia Minor, and everyone, absolutely everyone heard the Word of God. It's incredible to look at the life of Paul and his companions and perceive how the Word gave them will, power, and authority to preach. It is the Word that makes the work of God grow.

In those times, Paul and the disciples didn't have buses, trains, cars or airplanes to travel; neither did they have telephones, fax, computers, e-mail, laptop computers, and printers. They did not even have electric typewriters, telegrams, satellites, televisions, radios, newspapers or magazines. They could not depend on the Bible or any of today's modern technology. But they still reached a large geographic part, like Asia Minor, counting only on the disposition and the power of the Word of God. Today, we have everything that no one could ever have imagined. What are we doing for God? We should be ashamed and return to believing the Word like it really is: " *The Lord's message rang out from you not only in Macedonia and Achaia—your faith in God has become known everywhere"* (1 Thessalonians 1:8).

It's the faith in God's Word that causes positive results, and it is through the Holy Spirit that the Word is taken to every place. The simple faith in the Word is the secret to the victory of Christ's Church. Paul also acknowledged that it was the prayer of the Church together with the power of the Holy Spirit, working in unity, that would lead the word to be proclaimed: *"Finally, brothers, pray for us that the message of the Lord may spread rapidly and be honored, just as it was with you"* (2 Thessalonians 3:1).

It does not matter how much opposition we may have to encounter for the Word to be proclaim and glorified in Christ. In all parts of the world, the Bible is preached daily to millions of people in all imaginable ways and methods through men and women of God; whether it be through pastors, missionaries, evangelists, ministers or just simply church members that proclaim it in thousands of different languages and dialects fulfilling what the Lord Jesus said: *"And this gospel of the kingdom will be preached in the whole world as a testimony to all nations"* (Matthew 24:14).

"But God's word is not chained"

2 Timothy 3:2

In one street of an African country, a missionary from the American Bible Society held in his hands a New Testament. An African young man approached him and asked him if he could give him the little book. The missionary consented but felt curious to know the reason.

"Its pages have the perfect shape to make a cigar." The missionary impressed by the sincerity of the young man replied, "I will give you this little book if you promise that before making a cigar with these pages you will first read all the book. If not, I won't give it to you."

The African accepted his proposition and received the New Testament from the hands of the missionary. Fifteen years later that same missionary attended a crusade where a black evangelist would preach. When the evangelist saw the missionary, he approached him and asked him, "Do you remember me?

The missionary replied, "No. Did we meet before?

"Yes, fifteen years ago you gave me your New Testament with the condition that before I could make cigars with its pages I had to read it all. It took me some time to read from the Gospel of Matthew to John 13. While I read it, a deep conviction filled my heart, and I stopped smoking. So, I started preaching the Word. That New Testament is the reason why today I am here preaching. And he concluded saying to the missionary, "Thank you for the Word!" In short, the Word of God transforms the heart of man, taking away his addictions, saving him, restoring him; and then puts him in the position to preach the very Word of God. Halleluiah! God forms our character and our personality for us to be exemplary workers.

> *"He must hold firmly to the trustworthy message as it has been taught, so that he can encourage others by sound doctrine and refute those who oppose it".*

Titus 1:9

The Bible asserts us that the love of God is made perfect in us through the power of the Word of God. Do you want to have love? Search in the Word of God! The apostle John says: " But if anyone obeys his word, God's love is truly make complete in him" (John 2:5).

When Saul was ready to be anointed king of Israel by the prophet Samuel, Samuel said to Saul: "Tell the servant to go on ahead of us'—and the servant did so—'but you stay here awhile, so that I may give you a message from God" (1 Samuel 9:27). This verse drives us to an inevitable question: When was the last time you heard the voice of God through his Word? It's the Word that can give us direction. When we hear the Word of God, we are able to walk in his perfect will. We must desire and try to hear the voice of God, like that multitude that with great eagerness desired to listen to his Word: *"One day as Jesus was standing by the Lake of Gennesaret, with the people crowding around him and listening to the word of God..."* (Luke 5:1). We can say that today there are multitudes that desire to hear the Word of God and to learn from its pages. And those that hear and obey the Word of God become an active part of the family of Christ in any nation, race, people, color or language: *"My mother and brothers are those who hear God's Word and put it into practice"* (Luke 8:21).

The apostles made the preaching of the Word a priority in their ministries: *"So the Twelve gathered all the disciples together and said, 'It would not be right for us to neglect the ministry of the Word of God in order to wait on tables"* (Acts 6:2). Our priority in the ministry should be the preaching of the Word and no 'extra' activities that take its place. Pastors should try to appoint authority, like the twelve disciples in this occasion did, in order to be able to dedicate to the Ministry of the Word and to prayer. This is our call as ministers. We are responsible for taking the Word and for the quality of the messages that we are preaching.

A certain professor of homiletics use to say to his students in the seminar, "Every time I preach I receive credit just one sermon, while in reality, I am preaching four sermons in place of one." The students, not having understood what he was saying, asked, "But how can this be?" The professor replied, "Each time I preach I am really presenting four sermons. The first is the sermon I prepared before hand. The second is what I actually preach in public. The Third is what I do on the way home, which is always the best; and the fourth sermon is what the members of the church tell after hearing it, which, most of the time, does not have any association whatsoever with the other three." The people will always understand the message in a different way. Every head thinks in a different manner. We must have in mind that is very important to ask the Spirit of God to grant the people the necessary understanding to comprehend the message that is being announced. The Word will speak to each individual according to his need. As preachers, we should teach with simplicity so that everyone will understand. The ministry abides in the proclaiming of the Word. This way the primitive church worked, with the simple but powerful message of the Word. They proclaimed the Word in all the known parts of the world, in Jerusalem, as well as in Judea, Samaria and in the gentile world. *"The apostles and the brothers throughout Judea heard that the Gentiles also had received the word of God"* (Acts 11:1).

The book of Acts tells us, referring to Paul's first missionary trip, the proconsul Sergius Paulus was one the of the objective of Paul's preaching: *"The two of them, sent on their way by the Holy Spirit…proclaimed the word of God in the Jewish synagogues…the proconsul, Sergius Paulus. The proconsul, an intelligent man, sent for Barnabas and Saul because he wanted to hear the word of God"* (Acts 13: 4,5,7). So that means that people of high class and political positions seek and desire to hear the Word of God too. Closing, we can say that the Bible testifies that some of the most distinguished individuals of high political statuses want to hear the teachings found in its precious pages. In synthesis, the Word penetrates into the most intimate part of the human heart and transforms it because it has the power of a sword: *"And the sword of the Spirit, which is the word of God"* (Ephesians 6:17). Only the Word of God can change and transform the human heart and take it to a daily communion with its creator. Hallelujah!

The universe created by the Word of God

"By faith we understand that the universe was formed at God's command, so that what is seen was not make out of what was visible"

Hebrews 11:3

That is incredible! God spoke and everything came about, like David the psalmist declared: *"By the word of the Lord were the heavens make, their starry host by the breath of his mouth"* (Psalm 33:6).

In lecture number five of my series of studies of biblical eschatology (the study of the prophecies, which contain nineteen audio tapes, available only in Spanish), I declare without shame its title: Creation, not evolution. In this one-hour-study, I present dozens of biblical and secular proofs that destroy all the arguments of "false evolution." God is the creator and the source of all things. Now days, nuclear scientists, and scientist from all science fields, testify against the authenticity of the Scriptures and denounce the deceiving fallacy of illusive and the fraudulent theory of evolution. Archaeological proofs and innumerable sources verify the truth of the Word of God. Look at what the apostle Paul says to us in his second letter: *"But they deliberately forget that long ago by God's word the heavens existed and the earth was formed"* (2 Peter 3:5). What else does the Bible declare? That God is the supreme creator of the earth and the heavens and He is the reason for the existence of the universe, inhabited or uninhabited. He created man for his honor and for his glory. Peter says that: *"If anyone speaks, he should do it as one speaking the very words of God"* (1 Peter 4:11). We are called to speak about the power of the Scriptures and of the creative power of God that made all things.

The heathen and their relationship with God's Word

1 — The heathen mock the Word of God

> But they mocked God's messengers despised his words and scoffed at his prophets until the wrath of the Lord was aroused against his people and there was no remedy..."
>
> 2 Chronicles 36:16

We must be careful not to have any attitude of indifference to anything in relation to God's Word. We must always esteem and honor it. The same way, we must esteem also the preachers, ministers, and messengers of God. We must never treat the Word and the messengers of God with levity or indifference. God will surely judge everyone that disregards his holy Word.

2 — The heathen don't keep the Word and are indifferent to it

"They did not keep God's covenant and refused to live by his law"

Psalm 78:10

He that once had an experience with God but did not keep God's Word, going astray from his ways, his state has become worse than the first one. Be careful not to depart from the Word and maintain yourself in the way that God established.

"But grow in the grace and knowledge of our Lord and Savior Jesus Christ"

2 Peter 3:18

We are aware that there are millions of people scattered throughout the world that live indifferently to God's Word; but we also know that there are millions of persons that desire to grow in the knowledge of the Scriptures and in the wisdom of its counsel, which have illuminated and blessed people through several generations.

The apostle Paul had so much love for the Word of God and for the scrolls that he asked, in his letter to Timothy, his son in the faith, referring to imprisonment in Rome, the following statement: *"When you come, bring the cloak that I left with Carpus at Troas, and my scrolls, especially the parchments"* (2 Timothy 4:13). Charles Spurgeon, the great preacher of the Metropolitan Tabernacle of London, when he commented about this verse, once said: "Paul was a man inspired by God, but he loved the scrolls. He had already preached for thirty years, but he loved the scrolls; he had seen the Lord and had had a superior experience than the other men of God in his time, but he loved the scrolls. He had already been in the third heaven and had heard words incapable of being repeated, but he loved the scrolls. He had written the major part of the New Testament, but he loved the scrolls."

3 — The heathen reject the Word of God

"Therefore, as tongues of fire lick up straw and as dry grass sinks down in the flames, so their roots will decay and their flowers blow away like dust; for they have rejected the law of the Lord Almighty and spurned the word of the Holy One of Israel"

Isaiah 5:24

When you reject the Word of God, you will be under a curse; everything that you do will not succeed. When you reject the Word, you reject God also.

A certain pastor's friend took the Bible everywhere he went. Some people asked the pastor if this young man wanted to appear super spiritual. The pastor replied: "He does this, not because he feels strong spiritually, but because he knows how weak he is. He sinned many times for having ignored the Word of God, but now he is determined, by the mercy of God, to be steadfast in the Lord. He takes his Bible everywhere in order to always remember its counsel and not reject it anymore; because if he does he will again fall into the old ways of sin."

When Moses presented the Law to the people of Israel, he said that there was before them the way of life and the way of death. It would be life, if they obeyed the Word of God; death, if they disobeyed it. If you read Deuteronomy Chapter 28, you will see the consequences in the lives of those that chose to consider the Word and those that chose to reject it. Blessing or curses can overcome your life, depending on your attitude toward the Word. What will be your position; obedience or rebellion? You have free choice. Is a personal and private decision. Choose the Word...

These are rebellious people, deceitful children, children unwilling to listen to the Lord's instruction

Isaiah 30:9

4 — The heathen do not listen to God's Word

"Hear, O earth: I am bringing disaster on this people, the fruit of their schemes, because they have not listened to my words and have rejected my law"

Jeremiah 6:19

When you close your ears and your heart to the Word and you do not consider it and practice it, you are slowly being destroyed, until the enemy destroys everything that took God years to build in your life.

5 — The heathen forsake the Word of God

The Lord said, " It is because they have forsaken my law, which I set before them; they have not obeyed me or followed my law"

Jeremiah 9:13

The famous preacher G. Campbell Morgan had four sons that also became preachers. Howard, the youngest, has been known as a great preacher. Once, while his father was outside the city, Howard took his place in the pulpit. After the sermon, a brother asked him: "Who is the best preacher in your family?" Without hesitation, Howard replied: "My mother!" Sometimes, men and women that never reach the pulpit preach the best sermons, because they live with Christ daily, not leaving the Word of God aside like many others do. Only through the Word we will be an example to others.

6 — The heathen forget the Word of God

And because you have ignored the law of your God,
I also will ignore your children

Hosea 4:6

If I want my children to be ministers of the Word of God in the future, I have the duty and responsibility of being an example, persevering in my faithfulness to the Lord. This way God will be faithful to my children. I will not forget of everything that He has done for mi and of his Word and his commandments. The Lord will fulfill the promise he made concerning our dear children. Don't forget God and He won't forget you. Seek him daily and you will always find him.

Billy Graham told that, at the start of his pastoral ministry, he was to visit some members of his church. When he arrived at the house of a certain family, he perceived that, through the windows' glass, he could see inside the house. He rang the doorbell and when he looked inside the home, he was surprised at what the saw: the members of his church were playing cards in the living room. When they heard the doorbell and saw the pastor's figure from the other side of the door, they rapidly, at supersonic speed, gathered the cards and hid them. They grabbed the Bible that was on the sofa and they placed it on the table just as Graham entered the door. They thought that he had not seen them and greeted him: "Good afternoon Pastor Graham, here we are all together, in family, meditating the Word of God in Psalm 23. Isn't it wonderful?" How horrible! They were not meditating on Psalm 23; they were playing cards. They chose to forget the Word of God and they even tried to deceive their pastor. Many will give an account for their hypocrisies toward God and his Word. We have time for many things except to read and meditate in the Word. May the Lord have mercy on us!

7 — The heathen blaspheme against the Word of God

"So that no one will malign the Word of God"

Titus 2:5

Many blaspheme, full of evil intentions, against the Word of God and against the Church. After God had delivered the three Jewish boys of the flames of the blazing fire, the King Nebuchadnezzar said: "Therefore I make a decree, That every people, nation, and language, which speak any thing amiss against the God of Shadrach, Meshach, and Abednego, shall be cut in pieces, and their houses shall be made a dunghill: because there is no other God that can deliver after this sort." The three young men were faithful to God, and God was faithful to them. These Hebrew boys knew the Scriptures and they would be blaspheming God if they had bowed before the idol of gold that the King had made.

8 — The heathen are ashamed of the Word of God

"If anyone is ashamed of me and my words in this adulterous and sinful generation, the Son of Man will be ashamed of him when he comes in his Father's glory with the holy angels".

Mark 8:38

Some are ashamed of Christ and his Word. If you are, He will also be ashamed of you on that day, when he comes back in glory. To avoid sharing the Word with your friends, classmates, neighbors and people that you know, is the characteristic of an embarrassed Christian. If because of shame or timidity you deny him, He will deny you also.

A certain brother was disappointed and sad because he tried to memorize Bible verses and could not do it. He felt ashamed of carrying the Bible in his hand without having its words memorized. He went to his pastor and told him: "I feel ashamed in saying that I'm a Christian because when someone asks me something concerning the Bible, I can't answer them because I don't have the ability of memorizing verses. I feel ashamed before believers and nonbelievers." His pastor, a very wise man, observing the sincerity of the young man, replied: "First of all, you should never be ashamed of the Word of God. Secondly, you should never be ashamed of being a believer in Jesus. And thirdly, have courage, because when you strain something in a strainer, it doesn't matter how much water you pour, you will never be able to hold it, contain it or retain it, but you will always end with a cleaner strainer... Right?"

Don't be ashamed of the Word. Everyday, it will cleanse more of your conscience and your thoughts. Don't be ashamed of Christ, and He will make you wiser everyday. If you have the same struggle as the brother that couldn't memorize the Scripture, pray to God and ask him to give you the ability to retain the holy words in your memory. God will always produce results and nothing will be able to frustrate his will: *"So is my word that goes out from my mouth: It will not return to me empty, but will accomplish what I desire and achieve the purpose for which I sent it"* (Isaiah 56:11).

The saved and their relationship with the Bible

1 — Thousands of persons love and read publicly the Word of God

"When all Israel comes to appear before the Lord your God at the place he will choose, you shall read this law before them in their hearing. Assemble the people — men, women and children, and the aliens living in your towns — so they can listen and learn to fear the Lord your God and follow carefully all the words of this law".

Deuteronomy 31:11-12

The Bible is read everyday in thousands of different places by millions of persons, in hundreds of thousands of different languages. When the word is read publicly, the people fear God and turn from their evil ways. That is why the evangelistic crusades that we do around the world, which attract multitudes of people, are so important. In this crusades thousands of thousands of people can hear the Word of God, simultaneously, in just one place.

"Then the king called together all the elders of Judah and Jerusalem. He went up to the temple of the Lord with the men of Judah, the people of Jerusalem, the priests and the prophets — all the people from the least to the greatest. He read in their hearing all the words of the Book of the Covenant, which had been found in the temple of the Lord. The king stood by the pillar and renewed the covenant in the presence of the Lord — to follow the Lord and keep his commands, regulations and decrees with all his heart and all his soul, thus confirming the

*words of the covenant written in this book. Then all the
people pledged themselves to the covenant".*

2 Kings 23: 1-3

The word produces repentance when it is read publicly. In the book of Second Kings we read that the people of Israel experienced a revival when they read *"all the words of the Book of the Covenant"* (2 Kings 23:2). When King Josiah heard the word of the book of the law, he humbled himself before the Lord and he set in his heart to obey the words of the covenant. The result of that encounter of the king with the wonderful book of the covenant became history. *"Neither before nor after Josiah was there a king like him who turned to the Lord as he did—with all his heart and with all his soul and with all his strength, in accordance with all the Law of Moses"* (2 Kings 23:25). Would you like to bring revival to your city? Return to the Word!

In July 1985, I visited again the communist countries of the so—called Iron Curtain. From there, I took a flight to the city of Vienna, Austria. There, without waiting any longer, while I was waiting at the airport, I kneeled down before my seat; and with tears in my eyes and with my Bible in my hand, I thanked God for the privilege of living in a free country where I can read his Word without having problems with the authorities and where I can read it publicly for everyone that desires to hear it. Some people, who passed by, did not understand why I was in my knees crying. One man approached me and asked me, "Are you all right? Are you sad?"

I answered the courteous man, "I am well and I am not sad; on the contrary, I am very happy for being free, for living free, for having and reading this Word in a free country. I cry of happiness for being free."

Thanks be to God for the free nation that the United

States is. Thanks be to God that my dear Brazil is a free nation too. Thanks be to God that all the countries in Latin America are free, with the exception of Cuba. But I think that some day my wife's country will also be free. God will save the Cubans (this is my desire and prayer), and I will wait for that day patiently. Give thanks to God that you are free, because you have the right to freedom of expression, and above all, because you have the liberty of carrying the Bible through the streets of your country.

> *"All the people assembled as one man in the square before the Water Gate. They told Ezra the scribe to bring out the Book of the Law of Moses...he read it aloud from daybreak till noon as he faced the square before the presence of the men, women and others who could understand. And all the people listened attentively to the Book of the Law. Ezra praised the Lord, the great God; and all the people lifted their hands and responded, "Amen! Amen!" Then they bowed down and worshiped the Lord with their faces to the ground... for all the people had been weeping as they listened to the words of the Law"*

> Nehemiah 8:1,3,6,9

The public lecture of the Word brings conviction of sin and transforms the hearts of those that hear it. It is for this reason that we believed in the evangelization of masses. When we preach the words openly, the Holy Spirit manifests his power, converting the hearts of the people who are present.

> *"Then Jeremiah told Baruch, 'I am restricted; I cannot go to the Lord's temple. So you go to the house of the Lord...and read to the people from the scroll the words of the Lord that you wrote as I dictated. Read them to all the people of Judah who come in from their towns.*

*Perhaps they will bring their petition before the Lord, and
each will turn from his wicked ways, for the anger and
wrath pronounced against this people by the Lord are
great'".*

Jeremiah 36:5-7

Andrew Young, the helper of Dr. Martin Luther
King, former ambassador of the United States before the
United Nations and, later, governor of the city of Atlanta,
was invited to give a graduation discourse in the
University of Maryland. During his speech, Young challenged the students to purchase a Bible and read it a chapter per day. He added before the public, without intimida-
tion: "Have absolute security that that won't harm you in
any sense; on the contrary, it will illuminate you and help
you to find the real purpose in life." And he finished his
oration saying: "It is better to invest fifteen or twenty dollars today buying a Bible, than to spend a hundred dollars
per hour on a psychologist tomorrow."

Many of today's problems would be solved, simply, if
men would seek in the Word of God the solution to their
afflictions. Fear, emptiness of heart, anxiety, guilt, lack of
peace in the homes and in personal life, loneliness and the
suicidal desire, all these are symptoms of the desperation
of the human heart without Christ. In him, you will find
the fulfillment and happiness through his holy words.
Through the lecture of God's Words you will have the necessary knowledge to live this life to the fullest, to live it
well and happily together with your family and the other
persons around the world.

A long time ago, I heard someone say that there was a
psychologist in New York City that welcomed his patients
with a smile on his face and a New Testament in his hand.
When the appointment was over, as the patient would rise

to leave, he would be surprised by what the doctor said: "I have the answer to your problem!" "Really, doctor?" the patient would exclaim. The doctor would answer, "Yes! Take this New Testament, read it, and it will solve your emotional, mental and psychological problems; for in its words you will find the cure for your soul, what I can't give you and what no psychologist on this earth can offer you".

The words of Jesus are full of compassion, love, tenderness and comfort. They can ease the tired and burdened hearts. The medical centers are full of patients with physical disorders; however, the real problem is spiritual. The spiritual sicknesses of modern man are the ones that don't let him live his life to the fullest, and enjoy what God can give him through the knowledge of Christ and the acceptance of His words.

One time, in a hotel room in Puerto Rico, a man was ready to commit suicide. Another young man, who had perceived what, was happening when he looked through the window of his room, knocked at the door in the exact moment the man was ready to fire the pistol he had pointing to his head. When he opened the door, the suicidal man forgot that he still had the pistol in his hand. Crying, this man told the youth that he was about to take his life because in the casino, the night before, he had lost everything he had in the card game, and there was no way out for him. The young Christian man took a New Testament out of his pocket and gave it to him saying: "This book will change your life, read it!" After some moments together, the man got on his knees and, crying, gave his heart to Christ. From that moment, he read the New Testament attentively. Years later, this man became a pastor. His church was ready to receive a young evangelist who, when he came, the pastor recognized: " you are the young man that gave me the New Testament I was about to commit suicide!" "Yes, it's me! God called me to the ministry, and today I am a preacher of his Word", the young man answered. It is wonderful to see what the power of the Word of God can do in the heart of the man that surrenders entirely to Christ.

2 — The saved must understand that the Word of God is impartial in all its judgments

The scriptures are impartial and do not favor anybody in all of its judgments. To God there is no group of "special persons"; we are all special and equal before Him. See the instruction of God in the book of Exodus: *"The same law applies to the native—born and to the alien living among you"* (Exodus 12:49). Moses clearly left the words of the Lord to the people: *"You are to have the same law for the alien and the native—born. I am the Lord your God"* (Leviticus 24:22).

Unfortunately, there are churches and ministries that possess double standards, and so, they are always approving the " powerful" people in the church. In these cases, the people in better financial situation are always privileged. Many pastor treat differently those that give a high amount of tithe. Nobody deserves "special treatment," because when we preach the Word, it should divide up everyone equally and not some only. The Word should reach all the congregation indistinctively.

"For the Lord your God is God of gods and Lord of lords, the great God, mighty and awesome, who shows no partiality and accepts no bribes"

Deuteronomy 10:17

He is always just. We should learn that there is no distinction among "categories" or groups of people in the church.

> *"Who shows no partiality to princes and does not favor the rich over the poor, for they are all the work of his hands?"*

Job 34:19

How many lawyers and judges sell themselves out and pervert justice? How may have been partial in the judgments? Read what the book of Proverbs teaches us: *"To show partiality in judging is not good"* (Proverbs 24:23). Let's pray for God to teach us how walk in divine justice, and not in our view of what justice is. This principle is laid throughout all the Scriptures:

> *"To show partiality is not good—yet a man will do wrong for a piece of bread".*

Proverbs 28:21

The Bible shows us that the leaders of the Early Church were aware of the discrimination problem among brethren; that's why they have been forceful in the teachings concerning this, so that the church, learning about the justice of God, would see others like a person worthy of respect and honor. For example, Peter, in his discourse at Caesarea, clearly indicated the position of the Lord concerning this topic: "Then Peter began to talk: 'I now realize how true it is that God does not show favoritism but accepts men from every nation who fear him and do what is right.'" Our human tendency is to impress with appearances, but God is not like that. We look at the outward person, whereas the Lord looks at the heart. The apostle Paul also knew how important that matter was and wrote about it repeatedly in his letters. Paul said the following to the church in Rome: *"For God does not show favoritism"* (Romans 2:11). To the church in Galatia, he outlined this principle: *"God does not judge by external appearances"* (Galatians 2:6). To the church in Ephesus he said: *"There is no favoritism in him"* (Ephesians 6:9). To the church in Colossia: *"Anyone who does wrong will be repaid for his wrong, and there is no favoritism"* (Colossians 3:25). To Timothy, his son in the faith, Paul affirmed him: *"I charge you, in the sight of God and Christ Jesus…to keep these instructions without partiality, and to do nothing out of favoritism"* (1 Timothy 5:21). James, writing to the churches of the twelve tribes of the dispersion, declared: *"My brothers, as believers in our glorious Lord Jesus Christ, don't show favoritism. But if you show favoritism, you sin"* (James 2:1,9). And, finally, Peter, to the churches of the strangers scattered at Pontus, Galatia, Cappadocia, Asia and Bithynia, addressed: *"Since you call on a Father who judges each man's work impartially, live your lives as strangers here in reverent fear"* (1 Peter 1:17). Among the brethren of the Early Church there was much discrimination, and we perceive that today, in our churches, is not so different. I desire that we would be able to learn with the teaching of the apostles and also with the history of a young preacher that I will tell you as we continue.

A recently graduated seminarian was invited to preach for his very first time one Sunday morning. He was the son of a well—known pastor, and that made him somewhat proud and pretentious in front of his "humble" classmates. Everybody knew him as a young man full of great expectancy and future in the preaching ministry. They knew that he made certain selections in his friendships and that he made exceptions among his colleges also; but he was a good young man anyway, according to his friends.

All of the ministerial body was invited to hear him. His parents would also be there. The expectancy was great to hear the "pastor's son" give his first official sermon after his graduation. He had been the best student, but his arrogant heart and his discriminating attitudes were at the top when he saw the "adults" present to hear him. His emotions betrayed him. When he was invited to the pulpit, he made his greeting very respectfully, but he became extremely nervous. When he viewed his "important" colleges, and also the "non-important" colleges to him, and all of the body of the Seminary together, his legs started to tremble and his hands started sweating. He knew he could not do any mistakes. When he opened the Bible, he realized that the outline of his message that he had prepared was not there. He had left it at his house. Fear overcame the "inexperienced preacher." Close to him, in the first seats, were his professors. Frightful to see that his sermon was not with him, without knowing what to say, he started to speak: "Um, in this morning…Um, in this morning I will, um…I will in this morning, um…in this morning I will…" (Everyone noticed that something was going wrong). The "preacher" continued: "Um, well…I will, then, in this morning…um, in this morning I will." Suddenly, with all the tenseness he had, he rested his arms in the pulpit, and being not aware, he pushed the platform made of transparent plastic in form of a cross until he fell out of the platform. Everything fell on an old lady who was a professor of bible geography. Extremely embarrassed and humiliated in front of everyone, he apologized to the old lady saying: "Pardon me professor, I am just too nervous." In order to lessen his nervousness, the old lady, knowing how he really was and that God had allowed that to happen through that situation in order to embarrass him before everyone, she replied amiably: "That's no problem, young man. You had already announced many times that this would happen when you said 'This morning I will, I will…in this morning and… in this morning I will…' I am to blame for not getting out of my place, having heard so many times you were coming. Finally, you ended up falling over me, with pulpit, Bible and a glass of water…except for the sermon that you were supposed to preach." May God deliver us from believing we are better than everybody else. Before God, we are all equal; never forget that. We are not great; the Lord is great!

> *"Great is the Lord and most worthy of praise; his greatness no one can fathom".*

Psalm 145:3

The prophet Isaiah says to us that the nations and we all are *"less than nothing"* (Isaiah 40:17). This what we are; we are less than nothing. You see now how great you are?

3 — Some are willing to die for the Word of God

> *"I, John, your brother and companion in the suffering and kingdom and patient endurance that are ours in Jesus, was on the island of Patmos because of the word of God and the testimony of Jesus".*

Revelation 1:9

It doesn't matter what we endure for the Word, we must suffer for it and face all oppositions that rises up against it. It will always triumph. John, the beloved disciple, was imprisoned in the Island of Patmos for preaching the Word "illegally" in the Roman Empire. He was chained and taken to that island to die. It was exactly there where God gave him the great revelation of the apocalypse. Thousands upon thousands of people, throughout history, from bible times until now, have suffered martyrdom for the cause of the Lord. Even now days, many are persecuted, tortured and prefer to die before denying Christ and His Word.

During Billy Graham's Conference in Holland, in 1983, I had the great privilege and honor of meeting brother Andres (known as the God's smuggler of Bibles to the countries of Eastern Europe), founder of the International Ministry of Open Doors. He is an extraordinarily courageous man; you probably know his books. During one of the many times that he took Bibles inside the Iron Curtain, while he crossed the frontier between Czechoslovakia and Poland in his car, the communist guard stopped him when noticing that his automobile was too low to the ground, almost touching the street floor. He asked for his passport and said,

"What is it that you bring in this car that makes it so heavy loaded?"

"Oh, nothing!" brother Andres replied. (The car was full of Bibles).

"Nothing!" the guard exclaimed doubting, " You don't bring anything?"

While the two talked, the guard observed at the passport, and looking at brother Andres, he asked, " Why are you so nervous?"

"Me?" , brother Andres answered, "I am not nervous?"

"Okay, I will have to check your car and verify why it's so heavy", the police officer added, indicating brother Andres to get out of the car so he could inspect it.

At that time, the Lord spoke to brother Andres and told him, "Get out and let the man examine the car."

"Examine it!", brother Andres said, "Lord, did you say to let him examine it?"

"Exactly", the Lord answered him, "Let him examine it."

Brother Andres prayed a "telegram" prayer before getting out of the car: "Oh, Lord Jesus, you gave sight to those that had none. Now, I ask you to take the sight of this man who has it...in the name of Jesus". When Andres was getting out of the car, the guard started checking the car thoroughly. He started with the seats, he opened the two doors, he looked under the rugs, he opened the hood of the car and looked everywhere; he opened the trunk and...found some boxes that were closed. He opened the boxes and...said:

"Get in your car! Here is your passport with the visa to enter Poland."

The Bible smuggler could not believe it.

"You mean I can enter?"

"Yes!", the guard answered, "Just one thing more. I found out why your car is so heavy; is because of the weight of the boxes that I examined. Take my advice: go with the greatest speed you can, if not, your tomatoes and lettuces inside the boxes will rot."

Our God is a God of miracles. He is the same today, yesterday and forever...Instead of seeing the Bibles, the guard regarded tomatoes and lettuce inside the boxes when he opened them. Thanks be to God for them that are willing to give their lives in order for the Word of God to be proclaimed in countries that are communist, Arab-Muslim, Buddhist, socialist, etc.

4 — Some people testify the Word of God in the times of affliction

You are my refuge and my shield; I have put my hope in your word

Psalm 119:114

In time of adversity, affliction, tragedy, crisis, disease and war, millions of people have put their trust, faith, and hope in the Word of God. I know some Christian veterans of war that have been in Vietnam in the decade of 1960 for the U.S army. They are men that have seen their friends die and they have survived extremely difficult times. I know a brother name Tommy, from Long Island, New York, who tells of remarkable experiences. Once, he saw his friends being massacred by the communists during a helicopter barrage, and all that he did was bow his head, with his New Testament in his hands, and pray on his knees inside the trench that God would save his life. He put his faith in God's Word, which says: *"Remember your word to your servant, for you have given me hope. My comfort in my suffering is this: Your promise preserves my life"* (Psalm 119:49-50). God is faithful! He does not fail and won't ever fail! It doesn't matter the situation that you are facing; in the difficult times, seek the Word of God. Open and read his promises for your life. They are real! Believe!

A young Christian sailor was in charge of the radio in a ship during World War II. He usually ended the day reading Christian lecture and with a prayer through the radio. One morning, very early, after he spent the night guarding, he read Psalm 23 and had the idea of transmitting it through the radio. The other ships were also hearing him. He read the Psalm carefully and when he reached the 4th verse, emphasizing it, he said with a knot in his throat, almost crying: "Even though I walk through the valley of the shadow of death, I will fear no evil, for you are with me". Continuing, he read in the 6th verse: "Surely goodness and love will follow me all the days of my life, and I will dwell in the house of the Lord forever". As soon as he finished reading, he was surprised when he heard, in the high seas, men from sixteen ships answering back through the radio, all together in one voice, to what he had read: "Amen, amen!"

What book is this that has given comfort, strength and hope to so many people in moments of affliction? What book is this that continues to be the best seller in the whole world, year after year? It's the Bible! The Book of books! The book that's unique! Centuries have gone by, but the Bible remains! Empires have risen and fallen and are forgotten; the Bible remains. Dynasties are birthed and later end; but the Bible remains. Kings are crowned and dethroned; the Bible remains. Emperors have decreed its destruction, but the Bible remains. Atheists criticize it, but the Bible remains. Agnostics reject it, but it remains. The unbeliever abandon it, but the Bible is the same. The "intellectuals" argue its inspiration, but the Bible remains. It has been thrown to bonfires and burned, but the Word remains. Many say that it will be abandon and forgotten, but the Bible remains...It will always remain, forever and ever.

5 — The word can cure your sickness

"If you listen carefully to the voice of the Lord your God and do what is right in his eyes, if you pay attention to his commands and keep all his decrees, I will not bring on you any of the diseases I brought on the Egyptians, for I am the Lord, who heals you".

Exodus 15:23

One of the names given to God in the Old Testament was Jehovah Rapha, which means Jehovah the Healer; in fact, this is one among other names of God revealed throughout Scripture. God is the one that heals us! If you are sick, believe in His Word and you will be healed. The Word of God has the power to heal you.

> *"He sent forth his word and healed them; and rescued them from the grave"*

Psalm 107:20

You must believe in the Word, and what is written in it. When the doctors give you a bad report, you must believe another: God's report. It is clear that God uses doctors, and I believe in them. Luke himself was a physician; "Our dear friend, Luke, the doctor, and Demas send greetings" (Colossians 4:14). Although I believe in doctors, I believe more in God than in doctors. God uses them for our benefit, but only God can work miracles. "Surely he took up our infirmities and carried our sorrows, yet we considered him stricken by God, smitten by him, and afflicted...and by his wounds we are healed" (Isaiah 53:4-5).

Your healing has already taken place on the cross at Calvary. The prophet Isaiah says: "we are healed". This is for today! He has already taken your sickness and disease. All you need to do now is believe in the word that declares that we are healed. Jesus fulfilled the Scripture:

> *"When evening came, many who were demon possessed were brought to him, and he drove out the spirits with a word and healed all the sick. This was to fulfill what was spoken through the prophet Isaiah: 'He took up our infirmities and carried our diseases'".*

Matthew 8:16-17

The evangelist, Matthew, affirms us that Jesus healed all the sick "with a word." It is the Word that heals! Believe! When the servant of the centurion was ill, the centurion himself said that the word of Jesus would be enough: *"The centurion replied 'Lord, I do not deserve to have you come under my roof. But just say the word, and my servant will be healed'* (Matthew 8:8). **"Say the word!"** The centurion knew that in the Word of Christ there was power to heal him. The centurion realized that just like in the natural world he had authority to give orders to his subordinates, Jesus, in the spiritual world, had power to heal the sick with His Word. What happened in this account according to the Biblical context? *"Then Jesus said to the centurion, 'Go! It will be done just as you believed it would.' And his servant was healed that very hour"* (Matthew 8:13). In another passage, the bible says that Jesus continued to do miracles and wonders among the people: *"Jesus went throughout Galilee, teaching in their synagogues, preaching the good news of the kingdom, and healing every disease and sickness among the people"* (Matthew 4:23). You are included in this picture. He wants to heal you for his honor and glory.

Restating Psalms 116, Paul wrote to his brothers in Christ at Corinth: *"It is written: 'I believed; therefore I have spoken.' With that same spirit of faith we also believe and therefore speak"* (2 Corinthians 4:13). In other words, he was saying: believe the Word of God in your heart, and He will work the miracle in your life. You must believe and then speak. Believe that you are healed and, then, speak by faith, and it will be so. In the book of Romans, Paul tells us: *"Consequently, faith cometh by hearing the message, and the message is heard through the word of Christ"* (Romans 10:17). Deposit your faith in the Word that declares: *"I am the Lord, who heals you"* (Exodus 15:26).

Once, a young Christian lady was very sick with tuberculosis. The doctors had already sent her back to her home to die because the medicine had no effect anymore on her. One night, reading the Bible, the young lady read a passage from 1 Peter that said the following: *"He himself bore our sins in his body...by his wounds you have been healed"* (1 Peter 2:24). She read and reread this verse, and the Holy Spirit of God spoke to her heart: "The same Jesus that bore your sins is the same Jesus that bore your sickness." At that instant, an extraordinary faith in the Word of God took hold of the heart of that young lady. Yelling, she called her mother, who was at the next room, she said " Mom, mom..." Running, her mother entered her room thinking that something had happened to her and asked, "What happened? What happened?" The young lady exclaimed: "I believe that Jesus bore my sickness on the cross, so, I am healed by the Word of God!" At that point, she started to get out of her bed of sickness, took off the probe she had on her body, and by faith in God's Word, she stood up and began walking. She came out of the room shouting of joy; her mother was amazed. She shouted "I'm healed! I'm healed! Halleluiah! The Word of God says I am healed." That young lady was actually healed and today she lives by the power of God's Word, because she put her faith in the Scriptures.

In our crusades, we have seen extraordinary miracles when the people place their faith, without doubting or unbelieving, on the simple Word of God.

A miracle

It was early morning, February 15, 1981, in the city of Sapiranga, in the state of Rio Grande do Sul, Brazil, when my brother Tayrone had a terrible accident with his automobile. His accident was so serious that they took him to the City of Porto Alegre because small towns, like Sapiranga or Novo Hamburgo, were not able to assists him in such a critical state. So, they transferred him to the intensive care unit at the capital city of Gaucha. The first day, the doctors said that they had already done what they could do for him. He should be transferred to a hospital that is more specialized and better equipped in order to treat his brain damage effectively. My father, Jesus Pujol, arriving to Porto Alegre, asked my mother and I to go to the Assembly of God Church, located on General Neto Street, to find a pastor to go and pray for Tayrone. Desperate, as we were, we sought aid in the house of the Lord. That marvelous day of February 15, 1981 was the day that the Lord had prepared for a "real conversion" in me. I grew up in church and sat on the Sunday school pews but had not yet had a "real" encounter with God.

We got there when the choir was singing "Glory, glory, alleluia, glory, glory, alleluia, Jesus comes conquering…" I ran to the altar and, with tears in my eyes, I gave my heart to Jesus. I repented from all my sins and asked God to have mercy on Tayrone, for he was at the verge of death. After the service, we went to the pastor's office. He knew our family and when we explained to him our affliction and necessity, he sent a brother with us to the hospital to pray for Tayrone, who was already in the state of coma. My brother remained in the hospital for a week. There, he developed double the tuberculosis he had. The left side of his body had been paralyzed, he had water in his brain, and when they transferred him to another hospital, he suffered a heart attack of almost three minutes and they resuscitated him with an electro convulsive therapy. But we knew that it was God Almighty who did not allow him to die without salvation.

He remained at the PCU hospital for almost sixty–seven days in a deep state of brain coma do to the blow he had received in the head from the impact of the accident. He had hit his head against a pole and left his car totally destroyed.

My dear parents, brothers in Christ, and all our family believed, prayed, and many fasted and experienced spiritual warfare to see the miracle happen. Our faith was tested many times and in many ways during those seventy-seven days that Tayrone was in coma. Dr. Ibraim, who was responsible for Tayrone, recommended us an atheist doctor who would extract the water from Tayrone's brain, but we would have to take my brother to Argentina. This doctor knew that we were Christians and that he would operate our brother, making it clear that God would not have anything do to with the surgery; what he did would be because of his ability. We decided that the operation would not happen! Some doctors said that Tayrone would not die, and my uncle advised my father to start preparing the grave.

The son of the owner of the company where Tayrone used to work before he experienced this incident came looking for my mother to offer his "help". He knew a "very good witchdoctor", but he needed a piece of Tayrone's clothing to do his "work."

This witchdoctor possessed fame of a "quack". My mother answered that the life of Tayrone was in the hands of the Great Healer, the Lord Jesus Christ. He was already in control of the situation! We trusted in Him and only in Him!

On the first week of the accident, I was invited to participate in the lady's service from the Assembly of God's Congregation in Porto Alegre in the Araca neighborhood. My mother was not able to attend, but I went. When I arrived, I noticed that I was the only young man among the sisters. A sister called Teresa, a great servant of God, who was handicapped, she was sitting with her back facing me; she raised her hand, without seeing me, and said " There is a young man here, and God is telling him that his brother's accident is not for his death, but that God may be glorified in him. Come to the front that sister Julia will pray for you." That is exactly what I did; I kneeled down and cried much. Sister Julia, who was a prophetess from God, in charge of the small congregation of Araca, gave me a long prophecy, from my birth until that moment and told me what God would do with me (know we see its fulfillment) and that my brother would not die, but that the Lord would be glorified in his life. I trembled before the presence of the Lord, and I will never forget her words: "Many will know me through this accident, and as for you, I will use you in a great way, for you will preach this gospel in the four corners of the earth for my Name's glory." It was in Araca, in this humble and small church, that I took my first steps "preaching" Fridays for the youth services. I will never forget the love of those brothers in Araca and of the Assembly of God Church organization in Porto Alegre, who helped us with much love, perseverance and prayer.

On the evening of April 21, 1981, almost sixty-seven days after Tayrone entered into brain coma, brother Lucas went at the hospital and prayed for him. Many pastors and brothers had done it during all those days. On the morning of April 22nd, Tayrone woke up miraculously from his state of coma. It was an astonishment to all the doctors and to those who understood the gravity of the accident.

By the power of God and by the healing power of the Name of the Lord Jesus, Tayrone awoke and opening his eyes, he sat in the bed and made signs with his hands and arms; which had the probes that nourished him. He then asked the nurse a piece of paper and a pencil, for he could not talk. He wrote that he was hungry and that he wanted to drink chocolate milk...Hallelujah! Can you imagine how astonished all the nurses that assisted him where?

All the personnel from the PUC hospital were amazed. The doctors and even the director of the hospital came to see what was going on. Dr. Ibraim could not believe it. They called my mother from the hospital, telling her what had happened. When she entered my bother's room, she was startled to see so many people in inside. Doctors, medical students, nurses and hospital maids went to see the Tayrone's incredible healing after being so many days in a state of cerebral coma. Everyone spoke about the great "miracle of God" in the life of the young 25 year-old who had come out of coma. Some said, "They are 'Hallelujah' Christians." "Yes, it is so", my mother answered everyone, with tears of joy in her eyes while she was hugging her son. He was looking at her, trying to remember something. Hallelujah! This is what God does. During all that time, we spoke the Word of God and confessed that Tayrone would be healed. The doctors reported one thing, but God reported another. The honor and the glory belong to our Lord Jesus Christ, who miraculously raised and healed Tayrone. He used this accident to save me at eighteen years of age, calling me to preach His Word to the entire world. This is what I have done and will continue to do. We can see God work many wonders through simple faith in His Word.

Rev. Josué Yrión ministers God's Word with power at the Madras, India Crusade in August 1999.

Part of the multitude of 70 thousand people hearing the Word of God at the Madras, India Crusade.

Many testimonies of healing and deliverance after Rev. Yrión ministered at the Madras, India Crusade in August 1999.

Ghana Crusade, West Africa, August 2001.

Rev. Josué Yrión is an International Evangelist, for his age, his accomplishments have been quite remarkable. He has preached to millions of people in 70 countries in all the continents of the world, under the anointing of the Holy Spirit, drawing crowds into the saving knowledge of Christ. In 1985 he was in the Soviet Union and later in 1993 returned to preach in Russia at a Soviet military base in Moscow, where his ministry gave sixteen thousand Bibles away. He has received many honors, including the Congressional Medal and a Silver Badge with the recognition as an Illustrious Visitor and Son, by the government of Viña del Mar, Chile. He was the first Latin American minister ever to preach at Marina Beach in the history of Madras, India, where seven-

ty thousand people witnessed the power of God with signs and wonders. Josué Yrión, an ordained minister with the General Council of the Assemblies of God of the United States, is the Founder and President of Josué Yrión World Evangelism & Missions, Inc. Rev. Yrión lives with his wife Damaris and their two children Kathryn and Joshua Yrión Jr. in Los Angeles, California.

For more information and a catalog of books, audio and videos available in English, Spanish or Portuguese, please contact us or go to our website: http://www.josuéyrion.org or write to us:

Josué Yrión World Evangelism & Missions, Inc.

P.O. Box 876018
Los Angeles, CA. 90087-1118
United States of America
Phone (562) 928-8892
Fax (562) 947-2268
E-mail: josueyrion@josueyrion.org